All Churches Be One

Grace D. Balogun

All Churches Be One
By Grace Dola Balogun

Copyright ©2014 Grace Dola Balogun

Contact Author at:
www.Gracereligiousbookspublishers.com
1-646-559-2533

Grace Religious Books Publishing & Distributors books may be ordered through booksellers or by contacting the publisher:

Grace Religious Books Publishing & Distributors, Inc.
New York
213 Bennett Avenue
New York, NY 10040

All rights reserved. No part of this book may be used or reproduced by any means, graphic, electronic, or mechanical, including photocopying, recording, taping or by any information storage retrieval system without the written permission of the publisher except in the case of brief quotations embodied in critical articles and reviews.

Because of the dynamic nature of the Internet, any web addresses or links contained in this book may have changed since publication and may no longer be valid. The views expressed in this work are solely those of the author and do not necessarily reflect the views of the publisher, and the publisher hereby disclaims any responsibility for them.

Grace D. Balogun

The author of this book does not dispense medical advice or prescribe the use of any technique as for treatment for physical, emotional, or medical problems without the advice of a physician, either directly or indirectly. The intent of the author is only to offer information of a general nature to help you in your quest for emotional and spiritual well-being. In the event you use any of the information in this book for yourself, which is your constitutional right, the author and the publisher assume no responsibility for your actions.

Soft Cover ISBN: 978-1-939415-26-4
Hard Cover ISBN: 978-1-939415-27-1

Library of Congress Control Number: 2014490485

Editing and Interior Design by CBM Christian Book Marketing
www.christian-book-marketing.com

Cover Design by Lisa Hainline www.lisahainline.com

Printed in the United States of America
Grace Religious Books Publishing & Distributors, Inc. New York

All Churches Be One

Jesus Christ's Priestly Prayer

"After Jesus said this, he looked toward heaven and prayed: 'Father, the time has come. Glorify your Son, that your Son may glorify you. For you granted him authority over all people that he might give eternal life to all those you have given him. Now this is eternal life; that they may know you, the only true God, and Jesus Christ, whom you have sent. I have brought you glory on earth by completing the work you gave me to do. And now, Father, glorify me in your presence with the glory I had with you before the world began. I have revealed you to those whom you gave me out of the world. They were yours; you gave them to me and they have obeyed your word. Now they know that everything you have given me comes from you. For I gave them the words you gave me and they accepted them. They knew with certainty that I came from you, and they believed that you sent me. I pray for them. I am not praying for the world, but for those you have given me, for they are yours. All I have is yours, and all you have is mine. And glory has come to me through them. I will remain in the world no longer, but they are still in the world, and I am coming to you. Holy Father, protect them by the power of your name -- the name you gave me --so that they may be one as we are one. While I was with them, I protected them by the power of your name – the name you gave me – so that they may be one as we are one. None has been lost except the one doomed to destruction so that Scripture would be fulfilled. I am coming to you now, but I say these things while I am still in the world, so that they may have the full measure of my joy within them. I have given them your word and the world has hated them, for they are not of the world any more than I am of the world. My prayer is not that you take them out of the world but that you protect them from the evil one. They are not of the world, even as I am not of it. Sanctify them by the truth; your word is truth. As you sent me into the world, I have sent them into the world. For them I sanctify myself, that they too may be truly sanctified. My prayer is not for them alone. I pray also for those who will believe in me through their message, that all of them may be one. Father, just as you are in me and I am in you. May they also be in us so that the world may believe that you have sent me. I have given them the glory that you gave me, that they may be one as we are one. I in them and you in me and I am in you. May they also be in us so that the world may believe that you have sent me. I have given them the glory that you gave me, that they may be one as we are one. I in them and you in me. May they be brought to complete unity to let the world know that you sent me and have loved them even as you have loved me. Father, I want those you have given me to be with me where I am, and to see my glory, the glory you have given me because you loved me before the creation of the world. Righteous Father, though the world does not know you, I know you, and they know that you have sent me. I have made you known to them, and will continue to make you known in order that the love you have for me may be in them and that I myself may be in them" (John 17:1-26).

Grace D. Balogun

Dedication

I dedicate this book to our Lord and Savior Jesus Christ. He is the one and only Head of the Church, the foundation of the Church, the Cornerstone, our Gracious Redeemer and our King of kings, the Lord of lords, and the God of gods. He came to this Earth and purchased the Church with His own precious blood. We are part of His body, His flesh and His bones. The one and only, the Husband of the Church, the Blessed Ruler of all the souls of humanity on Earth; who prayed on the night of His crucifixion and said, "My prayer is not for them alone. I pray also for those who will believe in me through their message, that all of them may be one, Father, just as you in me and I am in you"(John 17: 20-21a).

I dedicate this book also to all the believing Christians, scholars, adults, pastors, ministers, young adults, as well as people of all other religions who will read this book to gain the understanding and come to the knowledge that all the Churches in the one body of Christ must have one doctrine in order to be one body of Christ – let Churches be one as Christ is one in all the Churches.

All Churches Be One

"Joy to the Earth! The Savior reigns: let all their songs employ; while fields and floods, rocks, hills, and plains repeat the sounding joy, Repeat the sounding joy, repeat, repeat the sounding joy."
(Words of Isaac Watts, 1719)

Grace D. Balogun

TABLE OF CONTENTS

Dedication		7
Preface		12
1	Jesus Christ's Prayer For The Church	17
2	One Body of Christ – The Church	23
3	The Nature of the Churches	30
4	Water Baptism & Baptism of the Holy Spirit	37
5	The Sacrament of The Church	56
6	The Lord's Supper of The Church	62
7	The Old Testament Institution of Worship	69
8	Church Worship In The Old Testament	80
9	New Testament Worship Early Christians	98
10	Church Worship In The New Testament	111
11	Catholic Churches' Doctrinal Ministry	123
12	Apostolic Catholic Orthodox Churches' Doctrinal Ministry	133
13	Orthodox Churches' Doctrinal Ministry	138
14	Lutheran Churches' Doctrinal Ministry	141
15	Anglican Churches' Doctrinal Ministry	145
16	Episcopal Churches' Doctrinal Ministry	149
17	Presbyterian Churches' Doctrinal Ministry	152
18	Protestant Reformed Churches' Doctrinal Ministry	156
19	Presbyterian Churches' Doctrinal Ministry	160
20	Methodist Churches' Doctrinal Ministry	164
21	Anabaptist Churches and Mennonite	169

22	Congregational Churches	173
23	Baptist Churches' Doctrinal Ministry	176
24	Church of Christ Doctrinal Ministry	181
25	Seven Day Adventists	185
26	Pentecostal Churches	189
27	What Can Make All Churches Be One?	193
28	Why Do We Have Different Doctrine?	197
29	What Can We Do To Makes All Churches One In Christ	201
30	Who Is The Body of Christ?	206
31	Speaking In Tongues	213
32	Miracle of the Healing Power of Christ	219
33	What is Christ's Commandment to the Church?	225
34	Why Do Churches Condemn Each Other?	229
35	Churches Misinterpretation of The Work of Christ	236
36	Religion	243
37	Other Denominational Churches' Doctrinal Ministry	247
38	Denominational Churches Observed Holidays & Festivals	256
39	Summary	266
40	Prayer for the Churches	273
41	Song of Praise	278
42	Biblical Indexes	280
43	Bibliography	282

Grace D. Balogun

No more let sins and sorrows grow, nor thorns infest the ground; he comes to make his blessings flow far as the curse is found, far as the curse is found, far as, far as the curse is found.
(Words of Isaac Watts, 1719)

Preface

The Church:

The word Church in the New Testament means: "The called out ones." A gathering of people, which means in the Greek Language: *Ecclesia – Church*.

The assembling of the citizens for the purpose of the affairs of the people; it is also referred to one particular meeting. Church also called Saints separated to the worship and service of God. Church always means people, never a building or organizational, or corporate structure. "The assembly was in confusion. Some were shouting one thing, some another. Most of the people did not even know why they were there. If there is anything further you want to bring up, it must be settled in a legal assembly. After he had said this, he dismissed the assembly" (Acts 19: 32, 39, 41).

Church in the Hebrew language means "Synagogue," which also denotes the Israelites' sacred meetings. In the New Testament "Church" is used for the community of God's people.

Church means the body of Christ where Christ is the Head of the Church. The people of God, the Kingdom of God, the Temple of God, the Bride of Christ, and the Body of Christ. The Church was called the people of God, which can be summed up in the covenantal Scripture, which God the Father said, "Therefore, say to the Israelites 'I am the Lord, and I will bring you out from under the yoke of the Egyptians. I will free you from being slaves to them, and I will redeem you with an outstretched arm and with mighty acts of judgment. I will take you as my own people, and I will be your God. Then you will know that I am the Lord your God, who brought you out from under the yoke of the Egyptians'" (Exodus 6:6-7).

The Lord is saying that He declares the essential meaning and purpose of His covenant at Sinai where the Lord promised to redeem Israel from the bondage of slavery and adopt them as His people and be their God. Israelites in return must promise to do the will of their Redeemer. The emphasis here is that Israel was helplessly held in bondage by a force they could not hope to overcome. Only by the Lord their God could they be freed because of God's covenant with the patriarchs and His love for His people; He would indeed deliver them.

God's redemption of Israel from Egypt served as a major basis for the transfer of ownership of Israel to Himself. Israel was God's by creation and election and now by redemption. The Lord God Almighty said I will be their God and they will be My people – Therefore, the people of God are, consists of those in the Old

Testament and in the New Testament who responded to God's calling to faith and whose spiritual origin rests primarily on the grace of God through Christ Jesus our Lord. Speaking of the people of God transcended from the Old Testament and the New Testament, which brought out questions about the relationship between the Church and the people of Israel. The Old Testament and the New Testament are the continuity of each other by the plan, or according to the plan and the authority of God the Father, God the Son, and God the Holy Spirit.

The Church was first revealed in the Old Testament: "He was in the assembly in the desert, with the angel who spoke to him on Mount Sinai, and with our fathers, and he received living words to pass on to us" (Acts 7:38). The assembly in the desert refers to Israel as the people of God. Just as Moses led the assembly of the people in the Old Testament, Christ leads the assembly of the New Testament Church designated by Abraham's seed and the Israel of God stands in continuity with the assembly of the Old Testament; and like the Old Testament, the Church of the New Testament is in the desert. It is a pilgrim Church on a journey of faith to the Promised Land. For this reason we must never become too comfortable with life here on this Earth.

In order to make this point clear: "The Lord gave me two stone tablets inscribed by the finger of God. On them were all the commandments the Lord proclaimed to you on the mountain out of the fire, on the day of the assembly" (Deuteronomy 9:10). This connection, which speaks of the Church as the Church in the wilderness, offers the same idea that was inferred from the intimate association of words, viewed as pre-existent therein before the creation of Israel. The Church was established in the New Testament. The Church according to the New Testament is the eschatological Israel incorporating Jesus Christ the Messiah, which is a progression between Old Testament to the New Testament. What was promised to Israel has now been fulfilled in the Church through Jesus Christ, especially in the Spirit of New Covenant. "I will sprinkle clean water on you, and you will be clean; I will cleanse you from all your impurities and from all your idols. I will give you a new heart and put a new spirit in you; I will remove from you your heart of stone and give you a heart of flesh. And I will put my Spirit in you and move you to follow my decrees and be careful to keep my laws" (Ezekiel 36: 25-27). God the Father promises to restore Israel not only physically, but also spiritually; this restoration involves giving them a new heart that is as tender as flesh so that they will respond to God's Word. Also, God will put his Holy Spirit in them. This is the work of God that will encompass the New Covenant, which was established by Jesus Christ. Without the empowerment of the indwelling of the Holy Spirit, it is impossible for a person to have true life and to follow the ways of God. It is very essential that the Church – body of Christ - remain open to the voice and guidance of the Holy Spirit.

All Churches Be One

Joy to the world! The Lord is come: let earth receive her King; let every heart prepare him room, and heaven and nature sing, and heaven and nature sing, and heaven, and heaven and nature sing.
(Words of Isaac Watts, 1719)

Chapter One

Jesus Christ's Prayer for the Church

In the Book of John, Scripture speaks of Jesus Christ's prayer to the Father, "After Jesus said this, he looked toward heaven and prayed: 'Father, the time has come. Glorify your Son, that your Son may glorify you. For you granted him authority over all people that he might give eternal life to all those you have given him. Now this is eternal life; that they may know you, the only true God, and Jesus Christ, whom you have sent. I have brought you glory on earth by completing the work you gave me to do. And now, Father, glorify me in your presence with the glory I had with you before the world began.

I have revealed you to those whom you gave me out of the world. They were yours; you gave them to me and they have obeyed your word. Now they know that everything you have given me comes from you. For I gave them the words you gave me and they accepted them. They knew with certainty that I came

All Churches Be One

from you, and they believed that you sent me. I pray for them. I am not praying for the world, but for those you have given me, for they are yours. All I have is yours, and all you have is mine. And glory has come to me through them. I will remain in the world no longer, but they are still in the world, and I am coming to you. Holy Father, protect them by the power of your name – the name you gave me – so that they may be one as we are one. While I was with them, I protected them and kept them safe by that name you gave me. None has been lost except the one doomed to destruction so that Scripture would be fulfilled.

I am coming to you now, but I say these things while I am still in the world, so that they may have the full measure of my joy within them. I have given them your word and the world has hated them, for they are not of the world any more than I am of the world. My prayer is not that you take them out of the world but that you protect them from the evil one. They are not of the world, even as I am not of it. Sanctify them by the truth; your word is truth. As you sent me into the world, I have sent them into the world. For them I sanctify myself, that they too may be truly sanctified.

My prayer is not for them alone. I pray also for those who will believe in me through their message, that all of them may be one. Father, just as you are in me and I am in you. May they also be in us so that the world may believe that you have sent me. I have given them the glory that you gave me, that they may be one as we are one. I in them and you in me. May they be brought to complete unity to let the world know that you sent me and have loved them even as you have loved me.

Father, I want those you have given me to be with me where I am, and to see my glory, the glory you have given me because you loved me before the creation of the world. Righteous Father, though the world does not know you, I know you, and they know that you have sent me. I have made you known to them, and will continue to make you known in order that the love you have for me may be in them and that I myself may be in them" (John 17:1-26).

Jesus' prayer for His disciples and all the believers shows that our Lord has the deepest longings for His followers, both then and now. It is also a Spirit inspired example of how all pastors and ministers should pray for their people, to include how Christian parents should pray for their children. In terms of praying for those we love and that are under our care, our greatest concerns should be that they may know our Lord Jesus Christ and His Word intimately, that God the Father may keep them from the world, from falling away, from Satan and from false teaching, so that they may constantly possess the full joy of Jesus Christ. Thus, that they be holy in thought, deed and character and that they may be one in purpose and fellowship, as demonstrated by Jesus and God the Father.

Christ also prayed for believing Christians' protection, joy, sanctification, love and unity within the body of Christ – the Church - those who belongs to God, believe in Christ and that that are separated from the world. He wants them to obey the Word of God, and the commandment of Christ, and accept His teachings and preaching.

Our Lord prays for Himself and sanctifies Himself. Jesus Christ sanctifies Himself by setting Himself apart to do the will of God the Father to die on the Cross. Jesus suffered on the Cross in order that those who believe in Him might be separated from the world and set apart to for God forever. Our Lord and Savior Jesus Christ also prayed for the unity of all the body of Christ – and for the Church, which is spiritual unity. Unity based on living in Christ, knowing Him, and experiencing the love of the Father and the fellowship of Jesus Christ.

In that, believing Christians may lead others to Jesus Christ, that they may persevere in the faith and finally be with Christ in Heaven and that the love that the Father has for Jesus may be in them, so that they love Jesus with the same fervent love that the Father does, and that Jesus Christ, by His Spirit, may dwell in and with them. It is a special quality of life that believers receive when they partake of the essential life of God through Christ; this allows them to know God in an ever-growing knowledge and fellowship with the Father, Son and the Holy Spirit.

Jesus prayed for the sanctification of all the believers with the truth – sanctify means to make holy, to separate or set apart for the Lord. Jesus Christ, the evening before His crucifixion, prayed that His disciples would be a holy people, separated from the world and sin and the sin nature for the purpose of worshiping and serving God the Father.

He rules the world with truth and grace, and makes the nations prove the glories of his righteousness, and wonders of his love, and wonders of his love, and wonders, wonders of his love.
(Words of Isaac Watts 1719)

Chapter Two

One Body Of Christ – The Church

The body of Christ is the Church - this is very unique and it constitutes one of the most significant concepts of Christianity. "Just as each of us has one body with many members and these members do not all have the same function, so in Christ we who are many form one body, and each member belongs to all the others" (Romans 12:4-5). All the believers were given different gifts of grace, as well as inward desires or enablement or abilities given by the Holy Spirit to individuals in the congregation to build up God's people. However, one's primary gift does not exclude the exercise of any other of the gifts as need may arise.

The primary purpose of the word "body of Christ" is to demonstrate the interrelatedness of diversity and the unity within the Church, especially with reference to the spiritual gifts of believers. The body of Christ is the last Adam. "So it is written: The first man Adam became a living being, the last Adam, a life giving spirit. The spiritual did not come first, but the natural, and after that the spiritual." (1st Corinthians 15:45-46) which mean the new humanity of the end time that has appeared in history of this world. Apostle Paul used the word, body of Christ, as the new temple, which indicates the Church, as the body of Christ, which has a long way to go spiritually and is not yet complete until Christ returns.

John the Baptist was preaching in the wilderness and said: "I baptized you with water for repentance. But after me will come one who is more powerful than I, whose sandals I am not fit to carry. He will baptize you with the Holy Spirit and with fire. (Matthew 3:11). Fire in the biblical term represents the judgment of God. John the Baptist teaches that the work of the coming Messiah will involve baptizing those who believed in Him with the Holy Spirit, a baptism that gives great power to live and witness for Jesus Christ.

"Every tree that does not bear good fruit is cut down and thrown into the fire" (Matthew 7:19). The fruit that the Scripture was referring to here is the false teachers who outwardly appear to be good followers of the Lord Jesus Christ because inwardly they are ferocious wolves. Fruit of false teachers will be unwholesome characteristics evident in the lives of their followers. They will be professing Christians whose loyalty is more to personalities than to the Word of God. They worship the creature more than the Creator.

Let us also see what the Scripture reveals again: "He will punish those who do to know God and do not obey the gospel of our Lord Jesus. They will be punished with everlasting destruction and shut out from the presence of our Lord and from the majesty of his power" (2nd Thessalonians 1:8-9). It could also mean everlasting punishment from God or from the Trinity. Fire can be represented by the power of the Holy Spirit as a sign of purification from sin for God's children and those who believe and put their lives in Jesus Christ the true and only begotten Son of God.

"These have come so that your faith of greater worth than gold, which perishes even though refined by fire – may be proved genuine and may result in praise, glory and honor when Jesus Christ is revealed"(1st Peter 1:7). Apostle Peter 's emphasis throughout his letter to the Churches during the early Church is we are called to rejoice in our trials because remaining faithful to Christ in the midst of our problems will purify our faith and result in praise, glory and honor both to us and to the Lord Jesus Christ at His coming.

Canal Christians Scriptures reveals: "Brothers, I could not address you as spiritual but as worldly mere infants in Christ, I gave you milk, not solid food, for you were not yet ready for it. Indeed, you are still not ready. You are still worldly. For since there is jealousy and quarreling among you, are you not worldly? Are you not acting like mere men? For when one says, I follow Paul, and another, I follow Apollo's, are you not mere men" (1st Corinthians 3:1-4)? The Scripture says that one of the Corinthian Church problems was its attempt to experience God's blessings while refusing to separate itself from the world's evil ways. The leaders of the Corinthian Church were allowing professed converts to come into the congregations without forsaking their sinful nature activities, tolerating within their fellowship selfish ambitions of divisions, which is the world's philosophy, jealousy and quarreling as well as so many immoralities, tolerating lawsuits, idolatrous festivals and most importantly, rejecting the teaching of the Apostles. They failed to see the necessity of absolute truth, love and godly standards. Then, Spirit baptism is not uniformly equated with any particular gift of the Holy Spirit.

All Christians then and today experience, as well as receive, a sense of the presence of the Holy Spirit or the power many, many times after their conversion. This is called the filling of the Holy Spirit. Believers will continue to be filled with the Spirit empowerment again and again through their life after conversion, particularly during the time that they boldly proclaim the gospel of God. When that happens they will be filled more and more with the Holy Spirit. This is because they need the power of the Holy Spirit to witness, and proclaim, the Gospel boldly and to highly exalt of the name of our Lord and Savior.

The life of the true converted Christians must be under the control and rule of the Holy Spirit as the "norm" of Christians' experience, "because through Christ Jesus the law of the Spirit of sin and death. For what the law was powerless to do in that it was weakened by the sinful nature, God did by sending his own Son in the likeness of sinful man to be a sin offering. And so he condemned sin in sinful man, in order that the righteous requirements of the law might be fully met in us, who do not live according to the sinful nature but according to the Spirit. Those who live according to the sinful nature have their minds set on what that nature desires; but those who live in accordance with the Spirit have their minds set on what the Spirit desires" (Romans 8:2-5).

Apostle Paul is teaching us that spiritual life, is freedom from condemnation, and is a victory over sin and fellowship with God, which comes through union with Christ, by the indwelling of the Holy Spirit. The Law of the Spirit of life is the regulating factors, activating power and life of the Holy Spirit operating in the hearts of all believing Christians. Whereby, the Holy Spirit is helping all believers to live a righteous life. Therefore, the Spirit given at baptism is an earnest down payment, guaranteeing the immeasurable blessings now, as well as more future blessings.

Water baptism is for the washing away of sins, washing of our rebirth just as a child was born, or came out of the womb and was wash clean from all the filthiness, dirtiness that he or she was in when in the womb. The baby became a beautiful baby is the same way with the renewal by the Holy Spirit. The Book of Titus: "He saved us, not because of righteous things we had done, but because of his mercy. He saved us through the washing of rebirth and renewal by the Holy Spirit, whom, he poured out on us generously through Jesus Christ our Savior so that, having been justified by his grace, we might become heirs having the hope of eternal life" (Titus 3: 5-7). God the Father supplies an abundant and adequate supply of His grace and power as a result of the new birth and the Holy Spirit's fullness in our life.

Grace D. Balogun

Thou didst leave thy throne and thy kingly crown when thou camest to earth for me; but in Bethlehem's home there was found no room for thy holy nativity: O come to my heart, Lord Jesus, there is room in my heart for three. (Words of Emily E. S. Elliott, 1864)

Chapter Three

The Nature of the Churches

The nature of the Churches is too broad, it cannot be exhausted in one word. It is very significant according to the New Testament Authors' descriptions. There are five biblical words that focus on the Churches, which need to be thoroughly analyzed: (1) The Kingdom of God, (2) The people of God, (3) The Temple of God, (4) The Bride of Jesus Christ, and (5) The Body of Christ.

The People of God

God the Father affirmed and emphasized the concept of the people of God, where God the Father summed it up in the covenantal word. "I will be their God and they will be my people" (2nd Corinthian 6:16). Therefore, the people of God are all those who are in the Old Testament and in the New Testament, those who responded in faith, who gave their life to Christ, and whose spiritual origin is exclusively in the gift of God's grace through

Jesus Christ our Lord and Savior. To make it clear to all the people in the world, both Jew and the Gentiles – the people of God consisted of those who are in the world yesterday, today, tomorrow and until Christ returns to set up His Kingdom. However, we must see the Church as a progression beyond the people of Israel; the Church must not be treated as a permanent replacement of Israelites.

The Kingdom of God

In terms of the Kingdom of God, many Christians in this present time maintained that the life of Jesus Christ, His death and His resurrection are the opening point of the Kingdom of God, which produced two ages. The Kingdom of God has already dawned; only it is not complete which the first aspect of it pertaining to Jesus Christ's First and Second Coming. In other words, the age to come has broken into this age and now the two ages exist one after another concurrently. It is very difficult to ascertain the relationship between the Church and the Kingdom of God, because the Church existed as a result of overlapping of the two ages. Christians may define the Churches as the appearance of the Kingdom through Christ.

It is very clear to all the believing Christians that the Churches are related and bound together with the Kingdom of God. On the other hand, the Church is not equal to the Kingdom of God. The Church and the Kingdom of God are related both as brothers. Our Lord Jesus Christ did not establish the Church, not until after His resurrection and ascension according to the New Testament; the Church was born on the Day of Pentecost. The New Testament speaks clearly about the Church, that the Church is in the teaching and ministry of Jesus Christ in general and in a specific ways. In general, Jesus Christ anticipated the official formation of the Church when He gathered to Himself His disciples and ordained them – they constituted the beginning of the eschatological Israel, the remnant that will believe in the Gospel. Jesus made Himself clear, and affirmed very well when He explicitly referred to the Church in the Book of Matthew (16: 17-19) where He promised that He would build His Church on this Earth and the gates of Hell would not prevail against it. Therefore, Jesus assured His followers with a promise of His ultimate success of His mission to the world.

Jesus Christ affirmed that the Church would overcome any forces of evil coincides with the idea that the Kingdom of God will prevail over its enemies and there will be intimate relationship between the Church and the Kingdom of God. Even though there is intimate relationship between the Church and the Kingdom of God, the Church and the Kingdom of God are not identified the New Testament does not equate the two. The fact is that the early Christians preached the Kingdom of God, not the Church. The New Testament identifies the Church as the people of the Kingdom not as the Kingdom; moreover, the Church is the key and the instrument of the Kingdom. Where the preaching of Apostle Peter on the Day of Pentecost, and the Church become the keys that opens up the Kingdom of God to all who would like to come in.

The Temple of God

The Old Testament anticipated the rebuilding of the Temple in the future Kingdom of God. "He brought me to the portico of the temple and measured the jams of the portico; they were five cubits wide on either side. The width of the entrance was fourteen cubits and its projecting walls were three cubits wide on either side" (Ezekiel 40:48). Jesus Christ said to the people that He will build such a construction which was fulfilled on the Day of Pentecost which witnessed the beginning of the fulfillment of the dream where the Holy Spirit inhabited the Church; the Temple was formed in all the believers' heart. There are many Scriptures in the New Testament that present the presence of the Holy Spirit in the Christians which constituted the new Temple of God; however, the temple is not yet complete; especially with the emphasis on the need for the Church to grow toward maturity in Jesus Christ which will be fully accomplished at the appointed time. But at this moment, Christians are as the Priest of God; they are to perform the service of sacrifice of praise to the glory of God. Read also Roman 12:1-2, and 1st Peter 2: 4-10 for further study of the Temple of God.

The Bride of the Church:

All those who believe in the Lord Jesus Christ and gave their life to Him are the Bride of Jesus Christ. The marriage of the Lamb - is applied to God and Israel in the Old Testament: "For your Maker is your husband – the Lord Almighty is his name the Holy One of Israel is your Redeemer; he is called the God of all the earth. The Lord will call you back as if you were a wife deserted and distressed in spirit a wife who married young, only to be rejected, says your God" (Isaiah 54: 5-6). God's people should not fear that their disgrace would continue forever, for God's judgment will soon give way to salvation. God would have compassion on His barren people and restore them to a place of favor in their own land.

The same is applied to Jesus Christ and the Church in the New Testament. Jesus is the Bridegroom. He has sacrificially and lovingly chosen the Church to be His bride. "Husbands, love your wives just as Christ loved the Church and gave himself up for her to make her holy, cleansing her by the washing with water through the word, and to present her to himself as a radiant Church, without stain or wrinkle or any other blemish, but holy and blameless" (Ephesians 5: 25-27). God has given the husband responsibility as the head of the household and the family. He must love His wife as Jesus Christ loved the Church and gave His life for her. Jesus Christ and the Church are like a marriage relationship between the believer and their Lord. Her responsibility during the betrothal time is to be faithful to Him.

"I am jealous for you with a godly jealousy, I promised you to one husband, to Christ, so that I might present you as a pure virgin to him"(2nd Corinthians 11:2). At the present time, the official wedding will take place at the appointed time and place and with the eternal union of Jesus Christ and His wife to be actualized. Jesus Christ, the Bridegroom, will take care of His bride the – Church.

Heaven's arches rand when the angels sang, in the claiming thy royal degree: But in lowly birth thou didst come to earth, and in great humility: O come to my heat, Lord Jesus, there is room in my heart for three. (Words of Emily E. S. Elliott, 1864)

Chapter Four

Water Baptism & Baptism of the Holy Spirit

John the Baptist was preaching to the children of Israel telling them that His baptism with water cannot be compared with the baptism of the Holy Spirit. Those who receive the baptism of water must be ready to receive the baptism of the Holy Spirit and fire, which means one baptism that consists of blessings and judgment. The Scripture revealed: "The Lord will wash away the filth of the women of Zion; he will cleanse the bloodstains from Jerusalem by a spirit of judgment and a spirit of fire" (Isaiah 4:4). The Scripture is telling us that those who will survive the coming judgment will be holy. They will have the character of God, who is the Holy One of Israel; they will be separated from the sinful world, cleansed from all defilement by Jesus Christ's blood and they will be regenerated by the power of the Holy Spirit.

Prophet Isaiah's prophesy was fulfilled on the Day of Pentecost; all those who believed represent the first fruits of purification from sin, but the baptism will not be completed until all the people experience the judgment at the Mercy –Seat which is the judgment seat of Christ. Many people misinterpreted the baptism of the Holy Spirit differently and conducted it differently, as well as apply it to believers in a different ways. Many Churches call it baptism of the Holy Spirit; some say baptism in the Holy Spirit. Where others called it baptism with the Holy Spirit; still some churches said, baptism by the Holy Spirit. But the fact is that the Holy Spirit is both the agent and sphere of baptism.

Our Lord Jesus Christ's baptism in the Holy Spirit: "For we were all baptized by one Spirit into one body – whether Jews or Greeks, slave or free – and we were all given the one Spirit to drink" (1st Corinthians 12:13). All believing Christians were all baptized by one spirit, which refers neither to water baptism nor to Christ's baptism of the believer in the Holy Spirit, such as occurred on the Day of Pentecost. Rather it refers to the Spirit's baptizing all the believers into Christ's body. Uniting them in the body and making them spiritually one with other believers; it a spiritual transformation that happens at conversion and puts the believer in Christ.

Baptism at conversion refers to the initiation, convocation of all believing Christians in the Church, which is the body of Christ. According to the John the Baptist, the people of his days long for the Messiah who is to come and that will baptize them with the Holy Spirit and fire. This prediction was fulfilled on the Day of Pentecost when the Holy Spirit descended to the Apostles and all the followers of Jesus Christ in Jerusalem like a fire of tongues purified all the believers and three thousand people were added to the Church, as well as were baptized on that day. The Holy Spirit blesses all and condemns all those who are unbelievers.

"I baptize you with water, but he will baptize you with the Holy Spirit" (Mark 1:8). John the Baptist was the first one who preached the Good News concerning Jesus Christ All those who accept Jesus Christ as Lord and Savior should proclaim that Jesus Christ is still the one who baptizes in the Holy spirit. The work of the Holy Spirit on the Day of Pentecost culminates with the Final Judgment.

We have to look at, "I would not have known him, except that the one who sent me to baptize with water told me. The man on whom you see the Spirit come down and remain is he who will baptize with the Holy Spirit"(John 1: 33). All the gospels emphasizes that Jesus Christ is He who will baptize with the Holy Spirit. This baptism was to be the sign and dynamic mark of those who love Jesus Christ. The Holy Spirit would be poured out on them so that they might carry on His saving work in all the nations of the Earth. This Scripture reflects the identical utterance of John the Baptist, but mentions again the baptism of the Holy Spirit.

"For John baptized with water, but in a few days you will be baptized with the Holy Spirit" (Acts 1:5). Jesus Christ Himself is the One who baptizes His believers in the Holy Spirit. Jesus told His disciples and prepared them to remember the prediction of John the Baptist that they will be baptized with the Holy Spirit, which will be a sign that will prepare them to ascend into Heaven;

referring back to John the Baptist's words and prediction will be fulfill after his ascension. Apostles witness the baptism of the Holy Spirit on the Day of Pentecost when the outpouring of the Holy Spirit arrived with power from Heaven. Apostle Peter reminded the people who were there from other countries, who spoke in other languages that this was the prophecy of Prophet Joel. "And afterward I will pour out my Spirit on all people. Your sons and daughters will prophesy, your old men will dream dreams. Your young men will see visions. Even on my servants both men and women I will pour out my Spirit in those days. I will show wonders in the heavens and on the earth. Blood and fire and billows of smoke. The sun will be turned to darkness and the moon to blood before the coming of the great and dreadful day of the Lord. And everyone who calls on the name of the Lord will be saved for on Mount Zion and in Jerusalem there will be deliverance as the Lord has said, among the survivors whom the Lord calls" (Joel 2:28-32). Prophet Joel envisioned that one of the primary results of the outpouring of the Holy Spirit will be the impartation and release of prophetic gifts. The manifestation of the Spirit through His gifts makes known God's presence among His people.

    Many years later Apostle Peter was sent to the house of Cornelius, the Holy Spirit manifested itself dramatically, just as the Day of Pentecost, which symbolized the beginning of the Gentile Pentecost. These events reminded Apostle Peter to reflect on Jesus Christ's words before His ascension and relay them to the Jewish

Christians leaders in Jerusalem when they wanted to know why he went to the house of the Gentile Cornelius. "Then I remembered what the Lord had said: John baptized with water, but you will be baptized with the Holy Spirit" (Acts 11: 16). The baptism of the Holy Spirit shows clearly that the Church was on the Day of Pentecost through the baptism of the Holy Spirit although as time goes on it was not mentioned that all the Corinthians believers had experienced dramatic, visible manifestation of the Holy Spirit when they were baptized.

It seems that they receive the baptism in water for the initiation rite, thus symbolizing repentance from sin and faith in Jesus Christ. This also signifies entrance into the communion with believing Christians and were incorporated into the body of Christ, which means a baptism in the Holy Spirit. This means they were in the stage in which the Holy Spirit would begin to operate in their lives. The Holy Spirit does not arrive or manifest to the believer in Corinth and today like the Day of Pentecost, or in no particular way or not in a dramatic way and not in tangible way.

Disciples experienced on the Day of Pentecost were completed because the disciples moved from the Old Testament covenant to the New Testament covenant. They through the most complex events in history, beginning with the crucifixion of our Lord Jesus Christ and His resurrection and His ascension, culminating with Christ's exaltation by sending the Holy Spirit which inaugurated the believers on the Day of Pentecost. The Scripture revealed that they Day of Pentecost was not the first time that the disciples first experienced the manifestation, or the presence of the Holy Spirit. "The Spirit of truth the world cannot accept him because it neither sees him nor knows him but you know him, for he lives with you and will be in you" (John 14:17). The Holy spirit is called the Spirit of Truth because he is the Spirit of Jesus Christ, who is the truth; and testifies to the truth enlightens concerning the truth, exposes untruth and guides the believer into all truth.

"And with that he breathed on them and said, receive the Holy Spirit" (John 20:22). Jesus Christ, before He ascended into Heaven, breathed on the apostles to receive the impartation of the Holy Spirit so that they could experience the regenerating presence of the Holy Spirit and the impartation of the new life in Christ. Baptism of the Holy Spirit was the second blessing or deeper experience of the Holy Spirit before conversion.

Pentecost was the second blessing to the disciples because they had been following Jesus Christ from the beginning of His ministry and after His crucifixion, death and resurrection. There is nowhere that the Scripture said that the Gentiles went through the second experience of the Holy Spirit. The Gentiles' Spirit baptism was concurrent with their conversion to Christ. Therefore, it shows clearly, and assured the believers of the level of the Christian's maturity or Christians' holiness. As the Corinthian church was not baptized in the Spirit, they had no experience of the two stages of baptism.

When this event happens, it is constitutive for a new level of a Christian experience of the presence of God. The Christian believers will know that the release of the Spirit power brought the expression of baptism in the Holy Spirit - the Spirit of God indwelling through the Holy Spirit at the moment of the Christian's salvation. As the Christians plunge into Jesus Christ, surrendering all to Him with repentance and strong faith, justification, and forgiveness, Sonship and public witness, the gift of the Holy Spirit and the seal of the Holy Spirit belongs to the Christian believers and all are part of initiation into the body of Christ.

We can see that some Christian churches use baptism in a different way to their congregations. Baptism with water means to plunge, immerse, sink, or wash: "Now Naaman was commander of the army of the king of Aram. He was a great man in the sight of his master and highly regarded, because through him the Lord had given victory to Aram. He was a valiant soldier, but he had leprosy. Elisha sent a messenger to say to him. Go, wash yourself seven times in the Jordan and your flesh will be restored and you will be cleansed. So he went down and dipped himself in the Jordan seven times, as the man of God had told him, and his flesh was restored and became clean like that of a young boy" (2nd Kings 5: 1, 10, 14). As Naaman, the Commander of the army of the Kings of Aram, who was plagued with Leprosy washed in the water and was cleansed from Leprosy, this baptism is a way to be immersed, thus by immersion in the water, means purification from all the filthiness of the body and Spirit or any uncleanness; it is therefore implying the act of purification from all that might exclude us, or make us unfit to be in the presence of God.

In the Old Testament when the Gentile seeking admission to the Jewish religion, they were required to submit to public repentance and acceptance of the Mosaic law which would be accompanied by immersion in the water that symbolized and effected the religious, moral, ritual cleansing from all defilements of paganism and worship of idols. This is the same as John the Baptist's baptism. Even though his baptism was challenged by the ruler of the synagogues and they needed an explanation from him as to his authority to perform his demand for purification of the children of Abraham; it was an offense to the Jewish rulers.

The Scripture reveals, "But when he saw many of the Pharisees and Sadducees coming to where he was baptizing, he said to them. 'You brood of vipers! Who warned you to flee from the coming wrath? Produce fruit in keeping with repentance. And do not think you can say to yourselves, we have Abraham as our father. I tell you that out of these stones God can raise up children for Abraham" (Matthew 3: 7-9). John the Baptist was telling the Jewish of his days that genuine repentance will be accompanied by the fruit of righteousness. True saving faith and conversion must become evident through lives that forsake sin and bear godly fruit. John the Baptist explained that baptism for repentance is needed to prepare the children of Israel for the coming of the Messiah. Jesus Christ himself being sinless was baptized and received a baptism of repentance, because of his ministry as a servant – the Messiah, was numbered with the transgressors.

"Therefore I will give him a portion among the great, and he will divide the spoils with the strong, because he poured out his life unto death, and was numbered with the transgressors. For he bore the sin of many, and made intercession for the transgressors" (Isaiah 53:12). God the Father Almighty promised to reward Jesus Christ for His atoning death, and Christ in turn promises to share His reward with all those who are strong in faith, who followed Him in doing battle against sin and Satan through the power of the Holy Spirit.

Whereby the assurance from the Father came clear to him when he came out of the water. As the Scripture revealed, "Here is my servant whom I uphold, my chosen one in whom I delight; I will put my Spirit on him and he will bring justice to the nations" (Isaiah 42: 1). The Father stated that the Messiah would be anointed with the Holy Spirit in order to perform His task of redemption.

The Scripture revealed, "I will proclaim the decree of the Lord: He said to me, 'You are my Son; today I have become your father" (Psalm 2:7). The psalmist begins by speaking of the people of Israel and the kings of this world who come against God's anointed Holy One, against God's law, His redemption, His Messiah and His moral teaching of His revelation. Jesus Christ knew that John the Baptist's ministry and work is from Heaven to identify him with an act of righteousness and to fulfill the Scripture.

Christ's assurance of His Sonship came with the power of the Holy Spirit descending upon Him for the work that the Father assigned Him to do on Earth. The Scripture revealed that Jesus Christ did not return to His own town of Nazareth, but was sent by the Holy Spirit into the wilderness, where He was tested and where He was prepared for His earthly ministry. He confirmed that the baptism of water assumed with the original association with the repentance and the remission or washing away our sin and with admission to the body of believers, it is also indicated that the gospel of God that came from John the Baptist, was the preaching of repentance of sin and water baptism. Christian baptism, conferring of the Holy Spirit begins from John the Baptist, with the exception of laying on of hands, before the Holy Spirit is conferred.

Believing Christians have to realize that Cornelius and his entire household, as well as all his people in his house have received the gift of the Holy spirit, which was Peter's justification for their baptism; the association of water baptism with the Holy Spirit possession gave rise to the baptism in or with the Holy Spirit. Baptism in the Book of Luke represents the expected response of hearing and receiving the gospel of God. Cornelius' household heard the Gospel and responded to the gospel of Jesus Christ as Christ, as the Lord and the Son of God. Irrevocable public confession of Jesus Christ as Lord, "That if you confess with your mouth, Jesus is Lord and believe in your heart that God raised him from the dead, you will be saved. For it is with your heart that you believe and are justified, and it is with your mouth that you confess and are saved" (Romans 10:9).

As the Scripture says, anyone who trusts in Him will never be put to shame. "For there is no difference between Jew and Gentile the same Lord is Lord of all and richly blesses all who call on him, for, everyone who calls on the name of the Lord will be saved" (Romans 10:9-13). God the Father also raised Jesus Christ from the dead. Furthermore, anyone that denies Christ's bodily resurrection cannot legitimately claim to be a Christian. He or she is still an unbeliever. For the death and the resurrection of Christ is the central event in salvation. The death and the resurrection in Christi is the central event in salvation. Commitment to baptism is included in all the privileges and obligations of the Christian life.

The Church must preserve the significance of baptism, without varying its conditions or abandoning its original practice, system and meaning. Today, some churches derive their own form of water baptism; some do not believe in water baptism at all. They will just use their hands to put the sign of the Holy Cross three times. Some will sprinkle the water on people's head three times and some will touch you with water three times in the name of Father, Son and Holy Spirit.

The original method of immersion and the accompanying confession of Jesus Christ's Lordship which clearly implies that the converting souls belong to Christ are no longer in practice in some Churches for example: "Or don't you know that all of us who were baptized into Christ Jesus were baptized into his death? We were therefore buried with him through baptism into death in order that, just as Christ was raised from the dead through the glory of the Father, we too may live a new life. If we have been united with him like this in his death, we will certainly also be united with him in his resurrection" (Roman 6: 3-5). Water baptism for the Christian represents his or her burial with Jesus Christ. Therefore, commitment to baptism comprises all of the privileges and obligations pertain to Christian life.

The good confession made at the baptism in response to the gospel of the suffering and risen Lord which was presented through the initiative of God and offered by faith, trust, and obedience is no longer necessary in many of the churches of God. Apostle Paul emphasized the link and the connection of baptism with the power endued by the Holy Spirit. Paul stated in the Scripture that -it is by one Spirit believers were baptized into the body of Christ – the Church, believers were made to drink of one Spirit, the Spirit of Christ, and sealed for the day of redemption by the same Spirit of God. As the Scripture said, "You however, are controlled not by the sinful nature but by the Spirit, if the Spirit of God lives in you. And if anyone does not have the Spirit of Christ. He does not belong to Christ. But if Christ is in you, your body is dead because of sin, yet your Spirit is alive because of righteousness. And the Spirit of him who raised Jesus from the dead is living in you; he who raised Christ from the dead will also give life to your mortal bodies through his Spirit, who lives in you" (Romans 8:9-11). All the Christian believers, from the moment of their spiritual birth and faith in Jesus Christ, have the Holy Spirit living in them. The life of Christian believers is not complete if they are not endued with the power of the Holy Spirit from above.

The water baptism is a cleansing of the Bride of the Church by the washing of water with the Word. To be clear and precise, the water, Word and the Spirit in this water baptism is a cleansing experience that can be seen as concomitant elements in a rite mediating to penitent hearts from the divine remission of sin. Apostle Paul was preaching to the Christians in the city of Colossae, professing that they don't need to be circumcised as some Jewish people were telling them to do. He said that in Christ, they were also circumcised by the putting off the sinful nature, not with the circumcision made by hands of men, but with the circumcision which was made by Christ having been buried with Him in baptism.

"In him you were also circumcised. In the putting off of the sinful nature, not with a circumcision done by the hands of men but with the circumcision done by Christ, having been buried with him in baptism and raised with him through your faith in the power of God, who raised him from the dead"(Colossians 2: 11-12). Circumcision was the sign that the individual Israelite stood in a covenant relationship with God. It symbolized a cutting away or separation from sin and all that was unholy in the world. Putting off the sinful nature, such circumcision is spiritual activity whereby Christ cuts away our old unregenerate nature of rebellion against God and imparts to us the spiritual or resurrection life of Christ.

Paul explained that circumcision cannot impart life, but portrays the change and the difference between baptism and circumcision. This is so that the believers were buried with Christ in baptism and they also were raised to new life in Christ's baptism with the extraordinary faith in the power of the Almighty God. A Christian's believing life and old ways are buried once and for all and from which a new life in Jesus Christ rises and emerges to a new quality way of living that appears with the Holy Spirit's direction, controlling and helping the believers to live a Christian life, which is the new life of Christ.

We can see this same life in the life of our Lord Jesus Christ where He offered Himself willingly for our sin. Christian believers who gave themselves to Christ have self-crucified themselves: "I have been crucified with Christ and no longer live, but Christ lives in me. The life I live in the body, I live by faith in the Son of God, who loved me and gave himself for me" (Galatians 2:20). The believer's relationship with our Lord and Savior should be in terms of a profound personal attachment to and reliance on his or her Lord. Those who have faith in Christ live their lives in intimate union with their Lord, both in His death and resurrection. They have crucified themselves to Christ; Christ lives His life through them. In the baptism, we must recognize that the moment we are converted, truly and indeed, publicly the believer takes up the Cross, is dying with Christ to self, to sin, and most importantly to the world, and rising with Christ to a new life constantly renewed by His resurrection power.

This death and the resurrection power of the Christians with Christ are implied in full acceptance of the gospel of God. The Scripture revealed that those who have truly gave their life to Jesus Christ, and those who are totally surrendered all to His Lordship cannot and will consistently accept Christ's death for their sins and act as if sin did not matter. Therefore, the repentant faith of the believer that holds salvation commits the believer; to a faith union with Christ in which the believer does with Christ to sin and rises with Christ to the renouncing of life of sin. Therefore, baptism expresses, illustrates, analyzes and finalizes the given of repentance and faith; the acts of baptism, which is irrevocable accomplishes all what it represents which is the full commitment to the Lord's possession, admission to the Church as part of the body of Christ. Therefore, giving empowerment of the Holy Spirit, remission and renunciation of all sins and worldly lust.

Apostle Paul made it clear that what is declared in baptism must be accomplished after the baptism. Christian believers must obey and be obedient to the commandment of the Lord; they must be loyal to the Church, the assembly of God that they join and they must also walk in the Spirit and bear more and more fruits of the Holy spirit. Counting themselves dead to sin, they must not let sin reign over them. Believing Christians who are baptized will rejoice greatly in what has happened to them, and maintain their baptismal behavior and characteristic for the remaining of their lives. Repenting deeply for every failure when they fall into sin of any nature. Baptism brought in the awareness of the Christian's conscience during the threat of persecution and Christians must meet it with good behavior. Baptism is a commitment to do good as one suffered for the Lord, but triumphed through the power of His protection.

Apostle Peter extends the interpretation of baptism to include a promise of social responsibility, assured support and protection now and in the world to come. And now in the face of evils that threaten the new believers, the eternal warfare of good and evil, help to escape the world under the judgment of God. An example of of this is Noah in the Old Testament where only 8 people were saved from the flood upon that sinful age. Although there is a firm assurance from that the Lord, that He has already overcome all the obstacles that can come through the life of believing Christians. According to the Book of John, the Scripture revealed that operation of the Spirit in baptism and the implied entrance to the Christian family are very clear: John insists more and more that it is necessary and that it is the baptism of the believers that matters.

John emphasized that without a new birth of water and Spirit, none can see or enter the Kingdom of Heaven, or attain a spiritual nature. He noted the healing of Jesus Christ of blindness by washing at the pool of Siloam: "He replied, the man they call Jesus made some mud and put it on my eyes. He told me to go to

Siloam and wash. So I went and washed, and then I could see" (John 9:11). John led the Church to call baptism the enlightenment – "Instead, one of the soldiers pierced Jesus' side with a spear, bringing a sudden flow of blood and water" (John 19:34). Nothing can be added to the finished work of our Lord Jesus Christ on the Cross; on the cross our salvation is completed. This suggested that one purpose of Christ's death was precisely to provide the water and the blood by which Christian believers experience would be transmitted and nourished. "This is the one who came by water and blood – Jesus Christ. He did not come of water only, but by water and blood. And it is the Spirit who testifies, because the Spirit is the truth. For there are three that testify the Spirit, the water and the blood; and the three are in agreement.

We accept man's testimony, but God's testimony is greater because it is the testimony of God, which he has given about his Son. Anyone who believes in the Son of God has this testimony in his heart, anyone who does not believe God has made him out to be a liar, because he has not believed the testimony God has given about his Son. He who has the Son has life; he who does not have the Son of God does not have life" (1st John 5:6-12). Everyone on this Earth should hear the Gospel because eternal life is in God the Son, the Lord Jesus Christ, and cannot be received or possessed in any other way. Jesus Christ is the only way and the life. Eternal life is Christ's life in believers. We have it as we maintain a vital faith relationship with Him. The continual witness of the Holy Spirit and sacraments is an ongoing experience of the Church, testifying that Christ has come to the world in our own form; He put on humanity and died on the Cross for our sin so that we might live with him in Heaven.

Christian baptism was therefore established and its spiritual significance and power was fully revealed through the power of the Holy Spirit. Christian baptism conveyed what it represents, which is the divine action in believing and receptive hearts of believers. Christian baptism preserves the covenantal basis for scriptural thoughts – God first offers in grace, humanity responds in gratitude, they don't deserve it. The Gospel, God offers through Jesus Christ the forgiveness, life, the Holy Spirit; the baptismal response which was hallowed by Jesus Christ and which expresses faith in the dying and rising with our Lord and Savior. Christians therefore die to former sinfulness and rise to newness of life. God fulfills for the believing heart all the promises of the Gospel to those who will receive the Holy Spirit. Therefore, in lieu of all of what baptism of the believers achieved, all the Christian churches must have one uniformity of the baptism, which is by immersion.

Grace D. Balogun

The foxes found rest and the birds their nest in the shade of the forest tree; but thy couch was the sod, O thou Son of God, in the desert of Galilee. O come to my heart, Lord Jesus, there is room in my heart for thee. (Words of Emily E. S. Elliott, 1864)

Chapter Five

The Sacrament of the Church

The heart of the expression of the Churches' Christian believers faith is the sacrament of baptism and the Lord's Supper. The first one symbolizes entrance into the Church. The second one provides Spiritual sustenance for the Church. The baptism of sinners symbolizes the sinner's entrance into the Church: the body of Christ. The Scripture revealed from the Old Testament initiated of baptism, especially in its association of repentance of sin and any form of sin.

"Then a man who is ceremonially clean is to take some hyssop, dip it in the water and sprinkle the tent and all the furnishings and the people who were there. He must also sprinkle anyone who has touched a human bone or grave or someone who has been killed or someone who has died a natural death. The man who is clean is to sprinkle the unclean person on the third and seventh days and on the seventh day he is to purify him. The person being cleansed must wash his clothes and bathe with water, and that evening he will be clean. But if a person who is unclean does not purify himself, he must be cut off from the community, because they have defiled the sanctuary of the Lord. The water of cleansing has not been sprinkled on them, and they are unclean. This is a lasting ordinance for them. 'The man who sprinkles the water of cleaning must also wash his clothes, and anyone who touches the water of cleansing will be unclean till evening. Anything that an unclean person touches becomes unclean, and anyone who touches it becomes unclean till evening.' " (Numbers 19:18-22). The Old Testament ceremonial cleansing is different from the New Testament cleansing. The blood of Jesus Christ in which, by faith and by repentance, cleanses all the people from all their sin, either knowingly or unknowingly.

Our Lord and Savior said, "I tell you the truth, no one can enter the Kingdom of God unless he is born of water and the Spirit. Flesh gives birth to flesh, but the Spirit gives birth to Spirit" (John 3:5). All the believers of Jesus Christ must be born again of water and the blood of Jesus. God gave His son as an offering for sin on the Cross. The atonement proceeds from the loving heart of God. Second, the baptism of John the Baptist anticipated Christian baptism; John the Baptist baptizes and administered the baptism of repentance in expectation of the baptism of the Spirit and fire that the Messiah would exercise. All those who give their life to Christ, who accept Jesus as Messiah will experience the baptism of fire and judgment. Third, the early Church practiced the baptism of initiation of the Lord Jesus Christ. "Then Jesus came from Galilee to the Jordan to be baptized by John. But John tried to deter him, saying, 'I need to be baptized by you, and do you come to me?' Jesus replied, 'Let it be so now, it is proper for us to do this to fulfill all righteousness.' Then John consented. As soon as Jesus was baptized he went up out of the water. At that moment heaven was opened, and he saw the Spirit of God descending like a dove and alighting on him, and a voice from heaven said, 'This is my Son, whom I love; with him I am well pleased' " (Matthew 3: 13-17). Our Lord Jesus was baptized by John for the following reasons: To fulfill all righteousness; after going through the waters of baptism, the heavens opened and the Holy Spirit descended to empower Him for the Kingdom ministry. Just as the Scripture said: "So he said to me, 'This is by the word of the Lord to Zerubbabel: Not by might nor by power, but by my spirit, says the Lord Almighty'" (Zechariah 4:6). In the Old Testament, the Kingdom comes not by human might or power, but by the Holy Spirit and his anointing.

"Then John gave this testimony: I saw the Spirit come down from heaven as a dove and remain on him. I would not have known him, except that the one who sent me to baptize with water told me, the man on whom you see the Spirit come down and remain is he who will baptize with the Holy Spirit. I have seen and I testify that this is the Son of God" (John 1: 32-34). The Scripture made it clear, the Gospel emphasized that Jesus Christ is He who will baptize with the Holy Spirit. This baptism was to be the sign and dynamic mark of the believers of Jesus Christ, which means that the Holy Spirit would be poured out on them so that they might carry on His saving work in all the nations.

These Scriptures prove further the truths about baptism. Baptism is intimately related to faith in God the Father, Son, and the Holy Spirit. Baptism stands as identification to the person of Jesus Christ with the death and resurrection of Jesus – baptism incorporates the person into the company of all the believing Christians. Sacrament is a religious ceremony recognized by all the Christians, or rite of passage that infers sources of blessings, and grace on people who receive it. Sacrament is recognized as of particular importance and is very significance. Baptism is an example of Sacrament in Protestant and Catholic Churches.

Catholic and Orthodox Churches teach that there are seven Sacraments to be observed: 1. Confirmation; 2. Baptism; 3. Holy Orders; 4. Marriage; 5. Confession, 6. Anointing of the Sick and the 7. Holy Communion. Roman Catholics teache that Sacraments are efficacious signs of grace, instituted by Jesus Christ and entrusted to the Church, whereby, divine life is dispensed to the believers. The visible rites by which the Sacrament is celebrated signify and present the grace proper to each Sacrament. It also bears fruit in those who receive it; Sacrament are necessary for Salvation. All the believing Christians recognized Sacrament as of importance and significance.

Sacrament is a Christian rite, just as baptism or the Catholic Eucharist; it is one of the important ceremonies of all the believing

Christians. It was ordained by Jesus Christ Himself; as a means of divine grace, as a sign, or symbol of a spiritual power.

Only two sacraments were recognized by the Churches': Baptism and the Lord's Supper; since these are the only ones ordained by Christ in the Gospel. Anglican sacramental theology divided as to the effects of the sacraments. Some hold views similar to the Roman Catholic concerning the outward ceremony and the inward grace is necessarily given. The other five sacraments are made by Roman Catholic officials, not by Christ and it was not in the Gospel.

Grace D. Balogun

Thou camest, O Lord, with the living Word that should set thy people free; but with mocking scorn, and with crown of thorn, they bore thee to Calvary: O come to my heart, Lord Jesus, there is room in my heart for three. (Words of Emily E. S. Elliott, 1864)

Chapter Six

The Lord's Supper of The Church

The Lord's Supper also biblically known as Communion: "Is not the cup of thanksgiving for which we give thanks a participation in the blood of Christ? And is not the bread that we break a participation in the body of Christ? Because there is one loaf, we who are many are one body, for we all partake of the one loaf" (1st Corinthians 10:16-17). The Lord's Supper is to be observed by all the churches of Jesus Christ in the world. It is a cup of thanksgiving; it is a cup of blessing was the name of the final blessing offered at the end of the common Jewish meal. It was this cup that Jesus Christ blessed at the end of this Last Supper with His disciples. Jesus Christ interpreted the Last supper as being the New Covenant in His blood; therefore, participation in the blood of Christ refers to the believing Christians sharing in the salvation provided by Jesus Christ's death and His resurrection.

Catholic churches called the Lord's Supper - "Eucharist;" in all other Churches around the world, the Lord's Supper is called,

"Communion Table." A prayer of thankfulness is always offered before partaking in the communion elements, where the breaking of the bread symbolizes Christ's spiritual nourishment of His Church as it celebrates the sacred meal during His earthly ministry. There are two scriptural truth that emerges on the Lord's Supper - the Last Supper was instituted by Jesus Christ Himself, "While they were eating, Jesus took bread, gave thanks and broke it, and gave it to his disciples, saying, 'Take and eat; this is my body.' Then he took the cup, gave thanks and offered it to them, saying, 'Drink from it, all of you. This is my blood of the covenant, which is poured out for many for the forgiveness of sins. I tell you, I will not drink of this fruit of the vine from now on until that day when I drink it anew with you in my Father's Kingdom" (Matthew 26: 26-29). This scripture described the Lord's Supper in four stages of the lives of believing Christians; it is very significant as it relates to the past, the present and the future.

Jesus Christ celebrated the Passover on the night before He was crucified. Passover is the holy and joyful festival that commemorates the Israelites' deliverance from the bondage of oppression of slavery. Four Cups corresponds to four expressions of redemptive promise by God: "Therefore, say to the Israelites, 'I am the Lord, and I will bring you out from under the yoke of the Egyptians, I will free you from being slaves to the Egyptians, and I will redeem you with an outstretched arm and with mighty acts of judgment. I will take you as my own people, and I will be your God, Then you will know that I am the Lord your God, who brought you out from under the yoke of the Egyptians. And I will bring you to the land I swore with uplifted hand to give to Abraham, to Isaac and to Jacob. I will give it to you as a possession. I am the Lord" (Exodus 6: 6-8). Therefore, the commemorative meal included the cup of wine which means for blessings, the second cup of Passover wine signified deliverance where there is singing, dancing as part of the festival of Passover meal; the third cup signified redemption, when God redeemed the Israelites. They were eating and rejoicing in the desert and the fourth cup of Passover wine signified Elijah's cup, which commemorates the fifth ceremonial cup of wine poured during the family Seder dinner on Passover day of the Israelites. The fifth cup is always left untouched in honor of Prophet Elijah, who according to prophesied will come back one day as an unknown guest to celebrate the advent of Messiah. The Jewish parents were expected to use the Passover to teach their children the truth of how God had redeemed them from slavery and sin and made them a special people under his care and control. Likewise, as the Lord's Supper, in the New Testament Christian believers Passover is designed to remind believers of salvation in Christ and our redemption from sin and satanic bondage.

It is a remembrance of Christ's death for the believer's redemption from sin and condemnation. Through the Lord's Supper we are once again confronted with the saving death of Christ and its redemptive significance for our lives. Christ's death is our ultimate motivation against falling into sin and for abstaining from all appearance of evil. It is a thanksgiving for the blessings and salvation of God, made available by Christ's sacrifice on the Cross.

The Present significance - the Lord's Supper is a fellowship with Christ and a participation in the benefits of His sacrificial death, as well as a fellowship with the other believing Christians who are the members of the body of Christ. In this Supper with the risen Lord, He, as the host, becomes present in a special way. It is a recognition and proclamation of the New Covenant by which believers of Jesus Christ reaffirm the Lordship of Christ and their commitment to do His will. Believers are to remain loyal, and to resist sin and to identify themselves with the mission that the he assigned for them to do.

The Lord's Supper is the - future significance - it is a foretaste of the future Kingdom of God and the future Messianic banquet when all the believing Christians will be with the Lord. The Lord's Supper looks forward to Christ's imminent return for His people and dramatizes the prayer for His Kingdom to come. At the Lord's Supper all the above mentioned were significant if they were made in a meaningful way. If we come before the Lord in true faith, sincere prayer and with commitment to God's Word and to God's will.

The Scripture revealed that, "It is we who extol the Lord, both now and forevermore. Praise the Lord" (Psalm 115:18). Jesus Christ introduced two changes into the Passover Seder. He equated his body with the bread of affliction and His blood, which was shed on the cross, with the cup of redemption. The second important aspect of the Lord's Supper in the early Church is that sometime some of them observed it weekly in conjunction with other feasts. The Lord's Supper through the New Testament involves the participation in Christ's salvation - believers are to do the Lord's Supper for the remembrance of Jesus Christ. "And he took bread, gave thanks and broke it, and gave it to them, saying, 'This is my body given for you, do this in remembrance of me. In the same way, after the supper he took the cup, saying, 'This is the New Covenant in my blood, which is poured out for you" (Luke 22:19-20). Jesus Christ announces the inauguration of the New Covenant based on His sacrificial death. The Scripture reveals and teaches that the New Covenant could only become valid by the death of Jesus Christ. The disciples entered in this new covenant when they were regenerated and indwelt by the Holy Spirit on the evening of Jesus' resurrection; and they were later baptized in the Holy Spirit on the Day of Pentecost.

Historically the Lord's Supper was to commemorate Christ's redemptive work of His death and resurrection - as the Passover was a remembrance of God's deliverance of Israel from slavery in Egypt. " This is a day you are to commemorate, for the generations to come you shall celebrate it as a festival to the Lord - a lasting ordinance for seven days you are to eat bread made without yeast. On the first day remove the yeast from your houses, for whoever eats anything with yeast in it from the first day through the seventh must be cut off from Israel" (Exodus 12:14-

15). The Passover feast was supposed to be an annual festival. Regular participation in the Lord's Supper for the New Testament Christians continues the prophetic significance of the Passover. In remembering of Jesus Christ's death and resurrection, Christian believers actualize its effects from past to the present. Moreover, the Lord's Supper anticipates Christ Jesus returning and with all the heavenly messianic, heavenly hosts with an immeasurable company of angels of the Kingdom of God. The most and very important significance of the Lord's Supper is that it involves and identified with the body of Christ, the people of faith. In reality in the New Testament Scripture, positively speaking the Lord's Supper symbolizes the unity and the fellowship of the believing Christians in the one body of Christ Jesus. "Therefore, whoever eats the bread or drinks the cup of the Lord in an unworthy manner will be guilty of sinning against the body and blood of the Lord. A man ought to examine himself before he eats of the bread and drinks of the cup. For anyone who eats and drinks without recognizing the body of the Lord eats and drinks judgment on himself" (1st Corinthians 11:27-29). Strictly warning no one should partake in the Lord's Supper unworthily they will face divine judgment.

All Churches Be One

When the heavens shall ring, and the angels sing, of thy coming to victory, let thy voice call me home, saying yet there is room, there is room at my side for thee. O come to my heart, Lord Jesus there is room in my heart for thee. (Words of Emily E. S. Elliott, 1864)

Chapter Seven

The Old Testament Institution of Worship

All the exodus and covenant at Mount Sinai reshaped the understanding of time and reordered Israel's life according to a new religious calendar. For example, they must observe one day out of seven days as holy to the Lord, which was established for the connection between the Sabbath and the original creation, "For in six days the Lord made the heaves and the earth, the sea, and all that is in them, but he rested on the seventh day. Therefore the Lord blessed the Sabbath day and made it holy" (Exodus 20:11). This law expressed God's nature and His disposition. For example it expresses His love, His goodness, His justice and His hatred of evil. The law also emphasized the eternal truth that obedience to God from a heart of love would result in a full life and in rich blessings from the Lord. God wants us to rest at least one day in a week after all our work. He is our Father in Heaven and He wants us to live a healthy life without stress. Rest in God's presence on the Sabbath day clarifies the goal of redemption in Old

Testament revelation - rest in God's presence in the land of covenant promise.

Sabbath worship of the holiness life for the children of Israel extended beyond, and it goes through the entire calendar year where six annual festivals observed as holy days established by Mosaic Law, including Passover, the Feast of unleavened bread, the Feast of First Fruits, the feast of Pentecost, the Feast of Trumpets, the Day of atonement and the Feast of Tabernacles. These great religious festivals and holy days corresponded to the major seasons of the agricultural cycle and acknowledge God Yahweh as their provider and sustainer.

Worship and observation of festivals that required pilgrimages of all the children of Israel, males to appear before the Lord at the Sanctuary Passover-unleavened bread, this form of worship reinforced the ideals of covenant, as well as reminded the Israelites of their physical and spiritual life solely depended upon the covenant love of God Yahweh. The Scripture says, "See, I set before you today life and prosperity, death and destruction. For I command you today to love the Lord your God, to walk in his ways, and to keep his command, decrees and laws; then you will live and increase, and the Lord your God will bless you in the land you are entering to possess. But if your heart turns away and you are not obedient, and if you are drawn away to bow down to other gods and worship them, I declare to you this day you will certainly be destroyed. You will not live long in the land you are crossing the Jordan to enter and possess. This day I call heaven and earth as witnesses against you that I have set before you life and death, blessings and curses. Now choose life, so that you and your children may live and that you may love the Lord your God, listen to his voice, and hold fast to him. For the Lord is your life and he will give you many years in the land he swore to give to your fathers, Abraham, Isaac and Jacob" (Deuteronomy 30:15-20). God the Father affirmed and commanded the Israelites and to us today ,believing Christians, to maintain their relationship with God by loving Him and listening to His voice. We must express our obedience; however, they had to recognize their inability to fulfill the law and thus they had to bring sacrifices of atonement for their shortcomings. Life and salvation were never promised as a reward for perfect obedience; the law assumed the imperfection of faith and obedience on the part of "God's people and therefore, he provided the sacrificial system that atoned for sin."

The Old Testament worship associated with King Solomon's Temple was worship that associated with the tabernacle rituals that were established by the Mosaic Covenant at Mount Sinai. This form of worship constituting, or consisting of confession, forgiveness and cleansing, enthusiastic praise, worship proper by lowering oneself before God and with a response of obedience with songs of praise, Temple service in the morning and in the evening, sacrifices. Passover, Pentecost, Tabernacles, and dedication feasts: including songs of Ascents, the prominent place of worship, of music, is the temple worship, which always with the priestly musical guilds, priests sacrificial liturgy.

Temples and Tabernacles were portable tent sanctuaries which were ordained by God and constructed by the children of Israel under the supervision of Moses. The Instruction and the design of the sanctuary as well as the directions for implementing the worship of God were part of the covenant revealed by God to Moses at Mount Sinai. All the direction and the design of the Tabernacle purpose was to show the imminence of God, the love of God, where God will live among His people. Scripture says, "Then have them make a sanctuary for me, and I will dwell among them" (Exodus 25:8). God gave instruction concerning the tabernacle's historical, spiritual and typological significance of the tabernacle, which must be based on what the Scripture says about the Tabernacle.

The Tabernacle was a sanctuary, a place set apart for the Lord to dwell among and meet with His people where we see God's glory over the tabernacle day and night. The very design and construction of the tabernacle as well as the prescriptions for worship performed, all reinforced the emphasis of Mount Sinai; between the divine immanence and the transcendence, that are principles of mediation to enter the presence of God. In the same way with the artistry and craftsmanship employed in the design and construction of the Tabernacle introduced the use of sign and symbol for inspiring worship, as well as conveying the education of God's people in majesty and holiness.

The High Priest supervised sacrificial worship [in the sanctuary officiated over the Day of Atonement ceremony handled the urim and the Thumnun, the peculiar objects. He made the breastpiece, in skilled work, in the style of the ephod, of gold, blue and purple and scarlet yarns, and fine twined linen. It was square. They made the breastpiece doubled, a span in length and a span in breadth when doubled. The priestly vestments was used to determine the will of God, in a certain issues. "He is to stand before Eleazar the priest, who will obtain decisions for him by inquiring of the Urim before the Lord "(Number 27:21). " About Levi he said, "Your Thummim and Urim belong to the man you favored. You tested him at Massah; you contended with him at the waters of Meribah" (Deuteronomy 33:8). After the people of Israel sinned by erecting the golden calf, the Levites stood with God even against their nearest relatives.

They held firmly to the covenant and chastened those who participated in the worship of the golden calf. The Aaronic priests officiated over sacrificial worship in the sanctuary under the direction of the High Priest led the congregation of the Israelites in corporate and festival worship. By transporting the Ark of the Covenant which served as religious educators and advisers to civic leaders and serves as a models of "When you are about to go into battle, the priest shall come forward and address the army," "The Israelites traveled from the wells of the Jaakanites to Moserah, There Aaron died and was buried, and Eleazar his son succeeded him as priest." "So Moses wrote down this law and gave it to the priests, the sons of Levi, who carried the ark of the covenant of the Lord, and to all the elders of Israel. "The Levite shall recite to all the people of Israel in a loud voice: Cursed is the man who carves an image or casts an Idol - a thing detestable to the Lord, the work of the craftsman's hands and sets it up in secret. Then all the people shall say Amen" (Deuteronomy 20:2, 10:8, 31:9, 27:14-15). According to the Scripture many sins of the Israelites were done in secret; therefore, they account for their sins individually which served as religious educators and advisers to civic leaders and serves as a models of Covenant obedience and holiness.

The Scripture revealed that: "The Lord said to Moses, speak to the priests, the sons of Aaron, and say to them 'A Priest must not make himself ceremonially unclean for any of his people who die, except for a close relative, such as his mother or father, his son or daughter, his brother, or an unmarried sister who has no husband for her he may make himself unclean. He must not make himself unclean for people related to him by marriage, and so defile himself" (Leviticus 20:1-4). This Scripture deals with the qualifications and standards for those who were to serve as ministers of God's people. They were to be examples of godliness both in their ceremonial duties and in their personal character and deeds; consequently God placed on them a higher standard than was required for membership among God's covenant people.

Solomon's temple witnessed the blessing of God's divine presence in the form of a cloud of glory. "And the priests could not perform their service because of the cloud, for the glory of the Lord filled his temple"(1st Kings 8:11). The glory of the Lord filled the temple after the Ark of the Covenant was brought into the

Temple. Where God's Word is living and is obeyed, there is glory of God's abiding from then and till now. And the abasement of divine abandonment as God's glory departed the temple due to Israel's sin of idolatry. "Then the glory of the Lord departed from over the threshold of the temple and stopped above the cherubim. While I watched, the cherubim spread their wings and rose from the ground, and as they went, the wheels went with them. They stopped at the entrance of the east gate of the Lord's house, and the glory of the God of Israel was above them" (Ezekiel 10:18). The glory of God left the Temple because of the people's sin and idolatry. God left His house reluctantly and gradually, but because of His holiness, He knew He had to separate Himself from the idolatry in the Temple. The sanctuary of the Lord is a symbol of God's presence in the midst of His people of Israel was retained in the shift from the desert tabernacle urban temple. "May the Lord our God be with us as he was with our fathers; may he never leave us nor forsake us" (1st King 8:57). King Solomon's prayer is an ideal model for what we should desire in our walk with the Lord. We should ask the Lord for His protecting presence and for his divine help. For our Lord and Savior, God the Father to confirm His Word by fulfilling His good promises for His work of divine grace in the believers' hearts to keep God's commands and to love His righteous ways; For God to answer our daily prayers and to supply our daily needs and to increase the believers understanding of God's great and awesome nature and for a heart fully committed to God and His will.

New theological scripture emphasis comes out through the Solomon's prayer of dedication, which included the Temple and made the Temple as the embodiment of the fulfillment of divine promises. Regarding King David's covenant and his kingship which made it clear that the Temple is a house of God as well as the house of prayer; the temple witness two historical things. The Temple witness the sovereignty of God over all His creations and at the same time as a token of the children of Israel covenant of obedience. The Temple also witness as the tangible reminder of God's transcendence - as a God who does not dwell in a house made by human hands. The Temple was characterized as a symbol of God's divine presence and a proof of His sovereignty and spiritual reality of the children of Israel.

The second temple that was dedicated to God Yahweh in Jerusalem after the Babylonian exile. The second Temple was a shadow of all the former temples; the Temple was restored, renovated and rebuilt with more expansion. It was the same Temple the infant Jesus Christ was dedicated by Joseph and Mary in which Simeon and Ana recognized baby Jesus as the expected Messiah. The same King Solomon's Temple, Jesus when he grew up cleansed so that the people will use it as a house of prayer. The Scripture revealed, "On reaching Jerusalem, Jesus entered the temple area and began driving out those who were buying and selling there. He overturned the tables of the money changers and the benches of those selling doves, and would not allow anyone to carry merchandise through the temple courts. And as he taught them, he said, 'Is it not written: My house will be called a house of prayer for all nations. But you have made it a den of robbers.' The chief priests and the teachers of the law heard this and began looking for a way to kill him, for they feared him, because the whole crowd was amazed at his teaching. When evening came, they went out of the city" (Mark 11:15-19). Jesus Christ drove those who were buying and selling in the Temple shows his zeal for true holiness and prayer among those who claim to worship God. Christ made it clear that God's house is a house of prayer; and it must be used for prayer, both Jews and Gentiles. The buying and the selling and money tables were taking place in the court of the Gentiles, whereby it made very impossible for the Gentile nations to pray in the Temple.

This was not how God set it up, or it was not God's command for the Temple; the Gentiles must not be defrauded of their place of prayer and worship as well as the Temple must be used basically as the house of prayer to God, where people communicate to God with everything they were going through in their lives. Also in this temple, Jesus Christ taught the people during His passion week before His crucifixion. This same temple was destroyed in A.D.70 according to Jesus' prophesy. The New Testament reveals that the sacrificial system associated with the Temple worship remained the Jewish religious experience of Jews all across the Mediterranean world on the Greek and Roman empire, whereby the spiritual sacrifices of prayer, fasting and giving of alms continues.

The Old Testament anticipates Christian worship in theological principal compared to children of Israel's worship. Demanding a response of the whole person, or people of God, as a creator and redeemer, encouraged congregational worship, which was active with participation from the worshipers. The focus of believing Christians should be on the redemptive activities of God in human history. All the worship of the Jews and the Gentiles is a symbol that enhanced worship, as well as improved worship didactically and observed a liturgical calendar; that the worshipers anticipated out of the ritual participation that was reenacted. Most important, was the life of obedience in the service to God's completion of worthy worship.

Grace D. Balogun

In the fifteenth year of the reign of Tiberius Caesar – when Pontius Pilate was governor of Judea, Herod tetrarch of Galilee, his brother Philip tetrarch of Iturea and Traconitis, and Lysanias tetrarch of Abilene during the high priesthood of Annas and Caiaphas, the word of God came to John son of Zechariah in the desert. He went into all the country around the Jordan, preaching a baptism of repentance for the forgiveness of sins. (Luke 3:1-3)

Chapter Eight

Church Worship in the Old Testament

The Old Testament worship is very important for two main reasons. The Scriptures are part of the New Testament Christians, which means that the Old Testament Scripture leads to the New Testament Scripture. The Old Testament Scripture is very valuable for the Christian church and serves as a divine and inspired revelation of God as the authoritative figure for the life of the body of Christ, which is the Church in theological principle and in teaching of the Scriptures . The Old Testament worship provided the pattern for the public and corporate worship, which was instituted in Judaism and in Christianity. Old Testament Scripture was from God the Father, the Creator of Heaven and Earth and everything that dwells in Heaven and on Earth and underneath the Earth. The Scripture revealed that, "In the beginning God created the heavens and the earth. Now the earth was formless and empty, darkness was over the surface of the deep, and the Spirit of God was hovering over the waters" (Genesis 1:1-2). This Scripture draws our attention to the fact of a real beginning.. God the Father had a plan in creation, and He will carry it out; God's process, His plans, and the role of the Holy Spirit, beginning from the creation were revealed in the Word of God.

The Old Testament worship emphasized the covenant of God's revelation and the redemptive work of God's actions in history of the world. He is worthy of our worship and devotion and adoration of the people of Israel for all that He has done for them. The mighty God of the Old Testament is holy, transcendent, inaccessible, mysterious in His ways, indescribable and inscrutable. The Scripture says, "Let them praise your great and awesome name he is holy. The King is mighty, he loves justice you have established equity; in Jacob you have done what is just and right. Exalt the Lord our God and worship at his footstool; he is holy.

Moses and Aaron were among his priests, Samuel was among those who called on his name; they called on the Lord and he answered them. He spoke to them from the pillar of cloud; they kept his statues and the decrees he gave them. O' Lord our God, you answered them; you were to Israel a forgiving God, though you punished their misdeeds. Exalt the Lord our God and worship at his holy mountain, for the Lord our God is Holy" (Psalm 99:1-9). Our Lord God Almighty is awesome and holy that even his name must be treated with the utmost reverence and respect. God should never be treated lightly, for he is enthroned far above humans in strength, justice , purity and greatness. We must both love and fear God, who is a holy God a God who dwells in a high and holy place, who is contrite and lowly in spirit. "For this is what the high and lofty one says - he who lives forever, whose name is holy: I live in a high and holy place, but also with him who is contrite and lowly in spirit, to revive the spirit of the lowly and to revive the heart of the contrite" (Isaiah 57:15) The Scripture says, God who lives in a high and holy place, promises to dwell with those who are contrite and lowly in spirit. Contrite spirit is referring to those who are brokenhearted because of their own sinfulness or the enemy's oppression and the person cries out to God for deliverance; those who are lowly in spirit, are those who humbled and mowed down by adversity God responds to the cry of such people in order to revive them with the light and life of His presence.

God our Father in Heaven deserves our worship because in His imminent presence, He is able to answer the prayer of those who call upon Him and forgive their past, present, and future sins. God the Father maintained an intimate relationship presence of a holy God that shows and heartfelt praises and worship as well as a desire for holy living among his people - Israel. "Speak to the entire assemble of Israel and say to them: Be holy because I, the Lord your God, am holy" (Leviticus 19:2). God the Father is telling the people of Israel and to all the believers, God's people today that they must be like Him. He calls them to express His divine nature by being separate from the ungodly customs and sins of the surrounding nations and by serving Him in love and righteousness. The same call of God the Father to holiness was first given to Adam and Eve in the Garden of Eden after they were created in God's image in order to reflect God's character. All the generations of Christian believers on this Earth must be imitators of God and be holy because our Lord and Savior is holy.

The God of the Old Testament is sovereign in all His creations. His sovereignty indicates and proves His absolute authority and power over all His creations for the purpose of His accomplishment of His divine will for the people of Israel. The God of Israel, Yahweh, will live forever and He will accomplish His sovereign will and plan among the nations of this Earth. "The Lord Almighty has sworn, surely, as I have planned, so it will be, and as I have purposed, so it will stand. I will crush the Assyrian in my land; on my mountains I will trample him down. His yoke will be taken from my people, and his burden removed from their shoulders. This is the plan determined for the whole world; this is the hand stretched out over all nations. For the Lord Almighty has purposed, and who can thwart Him? His hand is stretched out, and who can turn it back?" (Isaiah 14: 24-27).

The God of The Old Testament delivered the Israelites from the hands of their enemies; this shows clearly the holiness of God, The holy imminence of God, the sovereignty of God, and the divine uniqueness of God which constituted a call to worship the Lord God Almighty as our Redeemer King of the people of Israel. God the Father is majesty and perfect in character. He intervenes in all what is going on in the life of His worshipers and their experiences as they go through life differently.

The activity of God in human history served as a basis for Israel's worship and justification of the true worship of God, as recorded in the Old Testament as the foundational ideas of the Israelite's worship. In the Old Testament, God established His covenant promise by creating new revelatory relationships with the people of Israel when He said, " I will be your God," and covenant stipulations, " You will be my people." In this form, God established a special pattern of holy worship with the people of Israel. He designed and affirmed true worship as part of His redemptive work when He delivered the people of Israel from the bondage of slavery in Egypt. The Scripture described and affirms that the individual people of Israel were comprised of distinguishable by physical and spiritual elements without distinction between material and immaterial, the physical and the spiritual in the Old Testament.

According to the teaching of the Old Testament Scriptures, humans are indivisible individuals in spirit, soul and body; this is what makes a whole person; not just the immaterial essence of an individual, which means only flesh, this is where believers' blessing of the Holy name of God is proclaimed and worship. "Praise the Lord, O my soul; all my inmost being, praise holy name" (Psalm 103:2). The psalmist expresses thanksgiving and praise to the Lord for the benefits and blessings that He bestows on the believing covenant people of God; believing Christians must never forget God's goodness to them. To include all His blessings that the Lord God showered upon them through the Holy Spirit; they must be thankful at all times, every minute and every second. The understanding of the nature of the humanity by the Israelites is remarkably relevant for all the believing Christians today. It is also shows clearly those human beings are created in the image of God as an indivisible units. Also the acknowledgment of the interrelatedness of the physical and the spiritual dimensions in human being helps to prevent the establishing of the false teachers and affirmed work, play, and worship which are all the activities under the rule and will of a Sovereign God. Recognizing our unity of humanity allows the people of God to respond to God in true worship, in freedom to worship God with intellect, emotions, personality, senses and spirit soul and body.

The Old Testament worship fosters the notion of corporate identity, a sense of belonging to the unity of humanity - which means the worship of individuals finds its completion in public worship in a larger worship community or Church. "Let us not give up meeting together, as some are in the habit of doing, but let us encourage one another and all the more as you see the Day approaching" (Hebrews 10:25). The Day Approaching means the day of Jesus Christ's return for His pure bride is fast approaching. We must prove genuine faith which results in praises, thankfulness glory and honor when Jesus Christ is revealed. Worship of Abram during the patriarchal period was characterized as either an expression of praises or thanksgiving prompted by the manifestation of God in humanity, or the activity of Abram's obedience to divine directive. This means that Abram obeyed the commandment of God to move to Canaan. "So Abram left, as the Lord had told him; and Lot went with him. Abram was Seventy-five years old when he set out from Haran" (Genesis 12:4). The life of Abram from the very beginning emphasizes the truth that obedience to God is very essential to a saving relationship with Him. Abram obeyed the Word of the Lord. This type of worship took the form of building an altar, or sometimes prayer, or animal sacrifice. Other form of expressions of Abram worship included the building of a stone pillars and the pouring of drink offerings. "Early the next morning Jacob took the stone he had placed under his head and set it up as a pillar and poured oil on top of it. And this stone that I have set up as a pillar will be God's house, and of all that you give me I will give you a tenth" (Genesis 28: 18, 22). God Almighty came to Jacob with the message that the blessing promised to Abraham would be carried on through him, with this blessing came also to Jacob as God's blessings of His presence, His guidance and His protection. Taking a vows in response to a divine revelation, "Then Jacob made a vow, saying, 'If God will be with me and will watch over me on this journey I am taking and will give me food to eat and clothes to wear.' I am the God of Bethel, where you anointed a pillar and where you made a vow to me. Now leave this land at once and go back to your native land" (Genesis 28: 20, 31: 13). Ritual purification is indicated as, "So Jacob said to his household and to all who were with him, 'Get rid of the foreign gods you have with you, and purify yourselves and change your clothes" (Genesis 35:2). God directed Jacob's family to go to Bethel in order to bring them into closer obedience to His Word.

Furthermore, the circumcision was a sign of the covenant of obedience to God. "Then God said to Abraham, as for you, you must keep my covenant, you and your descendants after you for the generations to come. This is my covenant with you and your descendants after you, the covenant you are to keep: Every male among you shall be circumcised. You are to undergo circumcision, and it will be the sign of the covenant between me and you" (Genesis 17: 9-10). Abraham and his physical descendant were promised the land of Canaan. The covenant was everlasting from God's point of view. Circumcision was to be a sign and seal of God's covenant with Abraham and his offspring. It was a sign or mark that they had accepted God's covenant and God himself as their Lord. It was a seal of the righteousness that Abraham and his people had by faith. It was to remind the people of God's promises to them and their own personal covenant obligations: prayers and thanksgiving, petition and intercession. For further reading, please see Genesis 12:8, 13:4, 24:12, 25:21, 18:22-33, 20:7.

Job's worship as the head of his family offers sacrifices on his children's behalf. "When a period of feasting had run its course, Job would send and have them purified. Early in the morning he would sacrifice a burnt offering for each of them. Thinking perhaps my children have sinned and cursed God in their hearts.

This was Job's regular custom" (Job 1:5). As a godly parent, Job was deeply concerned for his children's spiritual well-being. He watched their conduct and lifestyle, praying that they would be kept from evil and would experience God's blessing and salvation. Job's practice of worship by confession and repentance is revealed in scripture as, "Therefore, I despise myself and repent in dust and ashes" (Job 42:6). In response to God's revelation, Job humbled himself in repentance means that Job considered himself and even his moral rightness as mere dust and ashes before a holy God. Job did not retract what he had said about his life of righteousness and moral integrity, but he did admit that his accusations and complaints against God were not appropriate for a finite human to make and he repented for doing so.

His petition and intercessory prayers are evident in, "So now take seven bulls and seven rams and go to my servant Job and sacrifice a burnt offering for yourselves. My servant Job will pray for you, and I will accept his prayer and not deal with you according to your folly" (Job 42:8-9). God called Job his servant, and acknowledges that he accepted Job's prayer. Job was fully restored to God's favor and was given spiritual authority with God. God always heard Job's intercessory prayer for his three friends because of Job's righteous standing with God. In the same way today, God the Father, answers the intercessory prayer of our Lord Jesus Christ and blesses us amazingly and immeasurable. "Ho, that I might have my request, that God would grant what I hope for, that God would be willing to crush me, to let loose his hand

and cut me off" (Job 6:8-9). Job established as a routine practice for Job which shows him as a blameless and upright man in the eyes of God. Its shows that Job feared and reverenced God with a life of obedience, which almost was equal to Abram's worship experience.

Moses' Worship

During the Mosaic era, the people of Israel's history and worship was recognized as religious worship that was shaped by moving from Egypt to Canaan. The covenant ceremonial worship at Mount Sinai was planned by God, established the divine Law for the people of God, especially the exodus from Egypt which God used to bind Israelite together as a worshiping people. The covenant ceremony at Mount Sinai resulted in a covenant that established and created the nation of Israel. The Scripture reveals, "Ask now about the former days, long before your time, from the day god created man on the earth; ask from one end of the heavens to the other. Has anything as great as this ever happened, or has anything like it ever been heard of? Have any other people heard the voice of God speaking out of fire, as you have, and lived? Has any god ever tried to take for himself one nation out of another nation, by testing, by miraculous signs and wonders, by war, by a mighty hand and an outstretched arms, or by great and awesome deeds, like all the things the Lord your God did for you in Egypt before your very eyes? You were shown these things so that you might know that the Lord is God; besides him there is no other. From heaven he made you hear his voice to disciple you. On earth he showed you his great fire, and you heard his words from out of the fire. Because he loved your forefathers and chose their descendants after them, he brought you out of Egypt by his presence and his great strength, to drive out before you nations greater and stronger than you and to bring you into their land to give it to you for your inheritance, as it is today. Acknowledge and take to heart this day that the Lord is God in heaven above and on the earth below. There is no other. Keep his decrees and commands, which I am giving you today, so that it may go well with you and your children after you and that you may live long in the land the Lord your God gives you for all time" (Deuteronomy 4:32-40).

The Mosaic worship warned the Israelites not to worship any foreign gods, or deities, and not to worship and form images such as idols. God affirmed that Him only should they worship and serve Him alone. Old Testament worship celebrates the Passover, which stands for exodus, supreme activities of divine judgment, divine deliverance, which grows to the development of Israelite's redemption. The purpose of the Passover animal sacrifice and other ritual atonement that was designed to remind the Israelites of the principles of God's holiness and His unique role as the Redeemer from human sins and sin nature, as well as the need for repentance, which led to the cleansing and renewal of fellowship within the people of God.

The Passover worship events exalted the covenant of God, Yahweh who redeemed the children of Israel from their enemies. "He did miracles in the sight of their fathers in the land of Egypt, in the region of Zoan" (Psalm 78:12). The Israelites failed spiritually because they forgot the deeds and miracles God had performed among their founding fathers. Likewise, we must not forget God's deeds and miracles done in and through the faith of the believers of the New Testament Church. Passover worship also reminded the children of Israel to the successive generations of the redemptive work of God that leads to inevitable worship of God in truth and in Spirit. "The Lord will reign for ever and ever" (Exodus 15:18).

The Mosaic Law which standardized the form of worship God worship as recitation for Israel which included liturgical responses such as Amen. "Praise be to the Lord, the God of Israel, from everlasting to everlasting. Then all the people said Amen, and Praise the Lord" (1st Chronicles 16:36). Hallelujah, sing praises to the Lord God Almighty. "It is good to praise the Lord and make music to your name, O Most High" (Psalm 92:1). Praise and thanksgiving are the basic elements in the believing Christian's life. We must give thanks to the Lord in the morning and in the evening for our salvation through His Son, Jesus Christ for His love and grace, and for His faithful guidance and care. We also express our gratitude for the Word of God and for all His spiritual gifts through the power of the Holy Spirit. "In the morning, O Lord, you hear my voice; in the morning I lay my requests before

All Churches Be One

you and wait in expectation" (Psalm 5:3). Believers must let God hear their voice firmly with determination to seek God with all their hearts, confidently knowing that God will hear their voice; He will persist in prayer and not live without it.

If believers orient their lives around God, morning prayers will be the natural thing to do. Each new morning calls for a renewed dedication of ourselves to God; fellowship with Him and feeding on His Word and wait in expectation for answers to our prayer, and throughout the day we will search for signs that God is at work in his life.

Vow and Oath Taking

"I will come to your temple with burnt offerings and fulfill my vows to you, vows my lips promised and my mouth spoke when I was in trouble. I will sacrifice fat animals to you and an offering of rams; I will offer bulls and goats" (Psalm 66:13-15). The reading and teaching of God's Law - "So Moses wrote down this law and gave it to the priests, the sons of Levi, who carried the ark of the covenant of the Lord, and to all the elders of Israel. Then Moses commanded them; At the end of every seven years, in the year for canceling debts, during the Feast of Tabernacles, when all Israel comes to appear before the Lord your God at the place he will choose, you shall read this law before them in their hearing, Assemble the people men, women, and children, and the aliens living in your towns so they can listen and learn to fear the Lord your God and follow carefully all the words of the Law. Their children, who do not know this law, must hear it and learn to fear the Lord your God as long as you live in the land you are crossing the Jordan to possess" (Deuteronomy 31:9-13). This verse explains the sacrificial worship as well as teaching the family the law of God. "The sons of Aaron the priest are to put fire on the altar and arrange wood on the fire" (Leviticus 1:7). Sabbath - "Remember the Sabbath day by keeping it holy. Six days you shall labor and do all your work, but the seventh day is a Sabbath to the Lord your God. On it you shall not do any work, neither you, nor your son or daughter, nor your man servant or maidservant, nor your animals, nor the alien within your gates. For in six days the Lord made the heavens and the earth, the sea, and all that is in hem. But he rested on the seventh day. Therefore, the Lord blessed the Sabbath day and made it holy" (Exodus 20: 20:8-11). Old Testament Sabbath was the seventh day of the week. To keep that day holy meant setting it apart as different from other days by ceasing one's labor in order to rest, serve God and concentrate on the things concerning eternity, spiritual life and God's honor.

Seasonal Festival:

"Three times a year you are to celebrate a festival to me. Celebrate the Feast of Unleavened Bread, for seven days eat bread made without yeast, as I commanded you. Do this at the appointed time in the month of Abib, for in that month you came out of Egypt

No one is to appear before me empty-handed. Celebrate the Feast of Harvest with the first-fruits of the crops you sow in your field. Celebrate the Feast of Ingathering at the end of the year, when you gather in your crops from the field. Three times a year all the men are to appear before the Sovereign Lord" (Exodus 23: 14-17). The Pilgrimage festivals Incense offerings and libations, "Aaron must burn fragrant incense on the altar every morning when he tends the lamps. He must burn incense again when he lights the lamps at the twilight so incense will burn regularly before the Lord for the generations to come. Do not offer on this altar any other incense or any burnt offering or grain offering, and do not pour a drink offering on it" (Exodus 30: 7-9). God gave a commandment about the burning incense, which symbolized the continual worship and prayer of God's people.

Penitential rites

"This is to be a lasting ordinance for you: On the tenth day of the seventh month you must deny yourselves and not do any work - whether native born or an alien living among you" (Leviticus 16:29). The Day of Atonement is included in the Penitential rites worship. Further purification rites are revealed as, "Then Aaron's sons the priests shall arrange the pieces, including the head and the fat, on the burning wood that is on the altar" (Leviticus 1:8). The Scripture revealed, "A tithe of everything from the land, whether grain from the soil or fruit from the trees, belongs to the Lord; it is holy to the Lord. If a man redeems any of his Tithes, he must add a fifth of the value to it. The entire tithe of the herd and flock - every tenth animal that passes under the shepherd's rod will be holy to the Lord" (Leviticus 27:30-32).

A tithe is a tenth of both the produce of the land and the livestock that was given to the Lord. The tithe of Israel was given to support the Levites, to assist in sacred meals and to aid the poor, the fatherless and the widows. And artistic responses in music were, "The priests then withdrew from the Holy Place. All the priests who were there had consecrated themselves, regardless of their divisions. All the Levites who were musicians:- Asaph, Heman, Jeduthun and their sons and relatives stood on the east side of the altar, dressed in fine linen and playing cymbals, harps and lyres. They were accompanied by 120 priests sounding trumpets. The trumpeters and singers joined in unison, as with one voice, to give praise and thanks to the Lord. Accompanied by trumpets, cymbals and other instruments, they raised their voices in praise to the Lord and sang; He is good; his love endures forever. Then the temple of the Lord was filled with a cloud, and the priests could not perform their service because of the cloud, for the glory of the Lord filled the temple of God" (2nd Chronicles 5:11-14).

Dance

"You turned my wailing into dancing; you removed my sackcloth and clothed me with joy" (Psalm 30:11). This prayer expresses the heartfelt cry of all believers who suffer affliction because of illness, trouble, or oppression from the world of the enemies of righteousness; it reveals that in times of deep trouble, we can hide in the shelter of God's presence.

Sign and Symbols

"Make the ephod of gold, and of blue, purple and scarlet yarn, and of finely twisted linen the work of a skilled craftsman. It is to have two shoulder pieces attached to two of its corners, so it can be fastened" (Exodus 28:6-7). The ephod was a loose fitting sleeveless garment extending to the knees; it was worn like an apron over the priest's robe. As high priest, Aaron represented the people before the Lord when he entered the Holy Place. In doing so, he foreshadowed Jesus our high Priest, who entered heaven to appear in his Father's presence as our representative.

Grace D. Balogun

Jesus, Our High Priest in Heaven

"And Jesus grew in wisdom and stature, and in favor with God and men" (Luke 2:52) We know that the Scripture did not say anything for eighteen years of Jesus' life during those years. We learn that he grew up in a large family, that his father was a carpenter and that Jesus learned the trade from His father. Joseph was not mentioned again in the Gospels; it is likely that Joseph died before Jesus began His earthly public ministry. Jesus provided for His mother and younger brothers and sisters.

Chapter Nine

New Testament Worship: Early Christians

Jewish form of worship is the roots of Christianity. The early Christianity could be easily traced from the Old Testament worship. The Scripture revealed three type of origin including the ethnicity and the institution of the synagogue. Early Christianity began with individuals that were fully Jewish. They converted as they were Jews to belief in Jesus Christ as the Messiah. Jesus Christ was a Jew from the city of Nazareth in Galilee; the twelve apostles and all other pillars of the Church like Barnabas and Paul were all Jews.

The Scripture revealed: "Jesus went up on a mountainside and called to him those he wanted, and they came to him. He appointed twelve designating them apostles that they might be with him and that he might send them out to preach and to have authority to drive out demons. These are the twelve he appointed: (Simon to whom he gave the name Peter); James son of Zebedee and his brother John (to them he gave the name, Boanergies which means Sons of Thunder); Andrew, Philip Bartholomew, Matthew, Thomas, James sonof_Alpheus, Thaddeus, Simon the Zealot and Judas Iscariot, who betrayed him. The mission and the purpose of Jesus Christ on Earth was to destroy the works of Satan and evil people, to release those who are in the bondage of oppression by Satan and sin.

When Jesus called and chose His twelve disciples, He gave them the power and authority to continue to do His battle against the forces of darkness. The Scripture revealed that Jesus, after he appointed his twelve disciples, He gave them authority to drive out demons from people; He did the same thing after He appointed the seventy two, and he gave them also the authority to overcome all the power of the enemy. The disciples were not only to go out and preach, but also to manifest the Kingdom's rule, power and authority by doing battle against Satan, driving out demons, and healing every kind of disease and sickness. "In those days Peter stood up among the believers a group numbering about a hundred and twenty) and said, Brothers, the Scripture had to be fulfilled which the Holy Spirit spoke long ago through the mouth of David concerning Judas, who served as guide for those who arrested Jesus. He was one of our number and shared in this ministry" (Acts 1: 15-17).

The day of the out pouring of the Holy Spirit, on the Day of Pentecost was fully accomplished when the Jewish event of the first missionary journey where the Jewish Christians, the first seventy that our Lord chose to preach the Gospel to the people of

Israel. Their main focus was the Jewish people. Christianity is from the Old Testament Scriptures to the New Testament when the coming of the Messiah was prophesied by the prophets. At the beginning of the early Christianity Old Testament was their Bible. Jesus Christ, during His earthly ministry, demonstrated by His word, and healing of miracles showing clearly that He is the promised Messiah, the fulfillment of the Old Covenant which was made for God's people - Israel therefore, the Old Testament was the source of biblical proof for the New Testament preaching and teaching.

Early Christianity was focused on Jesus as the Christ the fulfillment of the Old Testament Prophesy. During the early Church, the Jewish Christians writers of the New Testament called on the Old Testament people of Israel for instruction and exhortation. The Scripture reveals that, "For everything that was written in the past was written to teach us, so that through endurance and the encouragement of the Scriptures we might have hope. May the God who gives endurance and encouragement give you a spirit of unity among yourselves as you follow Christ Jesus. So that with one heart and mouth you may glorify the God and Father of our Lord Jesus Christ" (Romans 15:4-6). The Scripture is telling us that everything that was written in the past, in the Old Testament Scriptures is of utmost importance to the Christian's spiritual life. The wisdom and moral laws of God concerning every aspect of life, as well as His revelation concerning God Himself, salvation and Christ's coming all have a permanent value in the lives of all the people in the world. Moreover, they knew that the gospel of God through Jesus Christ, which was supposed to be the new Israel. "Therefore, the promise comes by faith, so that it may be by grace and may be guaranteed to all Abraham's offspring not only to those who are of the law but also to those who are of the faith of Abraham. He is the father of us all.

As it is written: "I have made you a father of many nations." He is our father in the sight of God, in whom he believed the God who gives life to the dead and calls things that are not as though they were. Against all hope, Abraham believed and so became the father of many nations, just as it had been said to him, so shall your offspring be. Without weakening in his faith, he faced the fact that his body was as good as dead - since he was about a hundred years old - and that Sarah's womb was also dead. Yet he did not waver through unbelief regarding the promise of God, but was strengthened in his faith and gave glory to God. Being fully persuaded that God had power to do what he had promised. This is why it was credited to him as righteousness. The words it was credited to him were written not for him alone, but also for us, to whom God will credit righteousness for us who believe in him who raised Jesus our Lord from the dead. He was delivered over to death for our sins and was raised to life for our justification" (Romans 4:16-25). Believing Christians were saved by believing in God's promises.

Two Biblical truths about the nature of saving faith should be noted; while one is saved through faith alone, the faith that saves is not alone. James states that faith without deeds is dead. Paul says it is faith expressing itself through love saving faith is a faith so vital that it cannot avoid the expressions of love for the obedience to the Savior and of serving others. Therefore, the Scripture comprised of two covenants, which stood as a continuous and single record of the divine redemptive work of God in human history.

For example, the form and the practice of worship of the early Christian may be found in the liturgy of the Jewish temple and in the synagogue. The Book of Acts of the apostles revealed: the first Apostolic Church gathered daily for worship in the Jerusalem temple and in the individual believers' homes where they devoted themselves to the service of God, and to the instruction in the Apostolic doctrine, fellowship, prayers and the Lord's Supper; given their example of Jesus, who worshiped in the synagogues and in the Temple. "He went to Nazareth, where he had been brought up, and on the Sabbath day he went into the synagogue, as was his custom. And he stood up to read" (Luke 4:16). During the early Church the apostles naturally retained temple worship, Sabbath keeping with the development of Christian worship patterns for Sunday, the day of resurrection of Jesus Christ. "On the first day of the week, every early in the morning the women took the spices they had prepared and went to the tomb" (Luke 24:1). Paul's evangelization of the Gentile world, which started from Greece, Asia, then Rome that the Church decided that the Gentile met with the Jewish Christians for corporate worship which is the Lord's Supper on the first day of the week - Sunday. "On the first day of the week we came together to break bread. Paul spoke to the people and, because he intended to leave the next day, kept on talking until midnight" (Acts 20:7). We find out, through the Scripture revealed that in addition to the weekly observance of the Lord's Supper, the New Testament records indicates worship in the apostolic church was the singing, reading of psalms, hymns, and Spiritual songs, prayer and fasting, alms giving, reading and teaching of the Old Testament and following the apostolic doctrine, also the manifestation of the gifts of the Holy Spirit.

For example, we have Paul's instruction on the spiritual gifts and an order of worship: "Now about spiritual gifts, brothers, I do not want you to be ignorant. You know that when you were pagans, somehow or other you were influenced and led astray to mute Idols. Therefore, I tell you that on one who is speaking by the Spirit of God says, 'Jesus be cursed,' and no one can say, 'Jesus is Lord,' except by the Holy Spirit. There are different kinds of gifts, but the same Spirit. There are different kinds of services, but the same Lord. There are different kinds of working, but the same God works all of them in all men. Now to each one the manifestation of the Spirit is given for the common good. To one there is given through the Spirit the message of wisdom, to another the message of knowledge by means of the same Spirit, to another faith by the same Spirit, to another gifts of healing by that one Spirit, to another prophecy, to another distinguishing between spirits, to another speaking in different kinds of tongues, and to still another the interpretation of tongues. All these are the work of one and the same Spirit, and he gives them to each one, just as he determines" (1st Corinthians 12: 1-11). The people of God were all baptized by one Spirit. Worship, where he specifically mentioned the singing of songs, studying of the Scripture, words of revelation, and tongues as well as the interpretation of tongues, which all comprise Christian worship till today.

During the early Church, the transition from Judaism to Christianity was not easy and it also creates problems and confusion for some Jewish believers in Jesus Christ, especially with the inclusion of the Gentiles. The letters of Apostle Paul established helpful guidelines, as well as tools and keys for resolving the problems associated with the practice of various Christian worship. The primary principles among them are the common good of the congregation gathered together for worship. "To prepare God's people for works of service, so that the body of Christ may be built up until we all reach unity in the faith and in the knowledge of the Son of God and become mature attaining to the whole measure of the fullness of Christ" (Ephesians 4:12-13). Paul indicates here that one of the purpose for which Christ gives gifted leaders a Church is for them to train, equip and prepare the whole body of Christ to do the work of ministry. The principle of conscience of individual accountability before the Lord Jesus Christ in certain matters, which related to freedoms and preferences of worship the Scripture revealed, " Accept him whose faith is weak, without passing judgment on disputable matters. One man's faith allows him to eat everything, but another man, whose faith is weak, eats only vegetables. The man who eats everything must not look down on him who does not and the man who does not eat everything must not condemn the man who does, for God has accepted him. Who are you to judge someone else's servant? To his own master he stands or falls. And he will stand, for the Lord is able to make him stand" (Romans 14:1-4). During early Christianity, the number of believers who are weak in faith were committed to eat only vegetables, many others were eating vegetables and all other foods, including meat. Paul was teaching that eating special food does not make one holy than the other person but the personal character, the love for God and obedience to His Word.

The main formation is the worship of the apostolic Church, ritual symbols of baptism and the Lord's Supper, the ceremonial baptism, which symbolized the cleansing from sin and sin nature, by Christ's redemptive work on the Cross, which also served as the initiation into the Church as the body of Christ. Also that some believers see it as public identification with Christ. "What shall we say, then? Shall we go on sinning so that grace may increase? By no means! We died to sin; how can we live in it any longer? Or don't you know that all of us who were baptized into Christ Jesus were baptized into his death? We were therefore buried with him through baptism into death in order that, just as Christ was raised from the dead through the glory of the Father, we too may live a new life" (Romans 6: 1-4). Water baptism for the Christian believers represents his or her burial and resurrection with Jesus Christ, but it is more when accompanied by true faith, baptism is part of our rejection of sin and our commitment to Christ, resulting in a continual flow of grace and divine life to believers. Christian baptism holds a great significance as a form of worship because it places the believers in a formal community or corporate worship - in the Church of Jesus Christ; it also signifies believers' newness of life in Jesus Christ and the Holy Spirit who instituted the Christians worship. The Lord's Supper symbolizes the believer's redemption through Jesus Christ just as the Passover meal in the Old covenant symbolized Israel's redemption in the wilderness exodus period.

The Lord's Supper described or depicts Christian redemption because Jesus Christ is our Passover Lamb and been sacrificed for us. The symbol of the Lord's Table or the Last Supper which comprises the centered elements of Christian worship because it represents the fulfillment of the Old Testament promises as activities of remembrance. It recalls the redemptive work of Jesus Christ; it also symbolizes Christian unity and fellowship; and it constitutes the Church's hope of Christ's return and the establishment, consummation of His Kingdom. "They sent their disciples to him along with the Herodians. Teacher, they said, 'We know you are a man of integrity and that you teach the way of God in accordance with the truth. You aren't swayed by men, because you pay no attention to who they are. Tell us then, what is your opinion? Is it right to pay taxes to Caesar or not?' But Jesus, knowing their evil intent, said, 'You hypocrites, why are you trying to trap me? Show me the coin used for paying the tax.' They brought him a denarius, and he asked them, 'Whose portrait is this? And whose inscription?' Caesar's they replied. Then he said to them, "Give to Caesar what is Caesar's, and to God what is God's" (Matthew 22: 16-22). God wants His people to obey the government rules and regulations. God ordained the government and all believing Christians must follow and obey the governmental laws.

Unity

The unity in the covenant, studied in the apostolic church by means of the fellowship meal feast that accompanied the observance of the Lord's Table. "In the following directives I have no praise for you, for your meetings do more harm than good. In the first place, I hear that when you come together as a church, there are divisions among you, and to some extent I believe it. No doubt there have to be differences among you show which of you have God's approval. When you come together, it is not the Lord's Supper you eat, for as you eat, each of you goes ahead without waiting for anybody else. One remains hungry, another gets drunk. Don't you have homes to eat and drink in or do you despise the church of God and humiliate those who have nothing? What shall I say to you? Shall I praise you for this? Certainly not" (1st

Corinthians 11:17-22)! The early Church believers were condemned by Paul because of their conduct. They were conducting themselves divisively and in an unworthy manner in the body of Christ at the Lord's Table. They were humiliating the members of Christ's body who were poor and who could not contribute to the meal were ignored and left hungry. Worship in the apostolic church consisted of many implications for worship and worship renewal in the contemporary Christian church.

For example, the worship that celebrates Christ have significant attention to the Lord's Supper and the value of the symbol of instruction and in worship. In the same way; worship in the New Testament that shows the corporate worship experiences must be balanced with form and freedom, structured worship that is provided by the Holy Spirit, which prompted the participation in the worship service; worship that explains the prophetic and anticipation of the Kingdom and testifies of Jesus Christ triumphs over sin and death and home for the realization of believer's heavenly worship of John's vision or prophetic vision as the Lamb of God who is enthroned in the Kingdom of God, the New Jerusalem. "Then I saw a new heaven and a new earth, for the first heaven and the first earth had passed away, and there was no longer any sea. I saw the Holy City, the New Jerusalem, coming down out of heaven from God, prepared as a bride beautifully dressed for her husband. And I heard a loud voice from the throne saying, now the dwelling of God is with men, and he will live with them. They will be his people, and God himself will be with them and be their God. He will wipe every tear from their eyes. There will be no more death or mourning or crying and pain, for the old order of things has passed away. He who was seated on the throne said, 'I am making everything new!' Then he said, 'Write this down, for these words are trust-worthy and true" (Revelation 21: 1-5).

God will wipe away every tear from the believers' eyes that the effects of sin, such as sorrow, pain, unhappiness and death of the loved one has caused. Evils will be gone forever, for the evil things of the first heaven and Earth have completely passed away. Believers although remembering all things worth remembering, evidently not remembering that which would cause them sorrow any more. The synagogue and early Christian worship where the synagogue was involved in some kind of informal gathering or the association of the Israelites during the Babylonian exile. New Testament Scripture revealed that the synagogue is a place of prayers, reading and teaching, studying and preaching of the Old Testament Scriptures, almsgiving, exhortation, and fellowship New Testament synagogues consisted of Jewish Judaism believers who were scattered through Palestine and under the jurisdiction of Jerusalem which is the center of the religious power of Judaism. It is also the site for the judgment and punishment in the matter of the Old Testament law.

All Churches Be One

"When all the people were being baptized, Jesus was baptized too. And as he was praying, heaven was opened and the Holy Spirit descended on him in bodily form like a dove. And a voice came from heaven; You are my Son, whom I love; with you I am well please." (Luke 3:21-22) Jesus, who was conceived and indwelt by the Holy Spirit is now personally anointed and empowered by the Holy Spirit for his Ministry.

Chapter Ten

Church Worship in the New Testament

The ultimate goal and the purpose of the Church is to worship God the Father, God the Son and God the Holy Spirit through Jesus Christ our Lord and Savior. The early Church knows that this is the reason for their existence. "For he chose us in him before the creation of the world. In love he predestined us to be adopted as his sons through Jesus Christ, in accordance with his pleasure and will to the praise of his glorious grace, which he has freely given you in the one he loves" (Ephesians 1:4-6). God the Father chose all those who believe in Jesus Christ. These are people who are destined to be holy and blameless in His sight. This is where God sees the salvation and the holiness of the body of Christ, certainly as entire body of Christ. Believing Christians maintain their personal living faith in Jesus Christ and persevere in union with Him. The Scripture also revealed in "You also, like living stones, are being built into a spiritual house to be a holy priesthood, offering spiritual sacrifices acceptable to God through Jesus Christ" (1st Peter 2:5). In the Old Testament the priesthood was restricted to the qualified descendants of Aaron alone. Their distinctive activity was to offer sacrifices and intercession to God on behalf of His people and to communicate with God. Now through Jesus Christ, every born again believer has been made a priest before God. The Priesthood of all believers means the following: The worship of the Church can be delineated by five aspects of the New Testament Church's worship - the first, the meaning of worship; second is the place of worship; third is the nature of worship; fourth the order of worship, the expressions of worship.

The Meaning of Worship:

The Scripture did not say specifically, and there is nowhere in the Scripture that gives a clarification or definition of how to worship and when to worship. Christians believers were left with the specific notion and general impression that says worship to God is to ascribe to Him the acknowledgment of His greatness as well as how He is worthy of our worship. He alone is worthy and deserves our worship. Worship is an attitude and an act of adoration; God is worthy of our reverence and our praises. In the Old Testament prophets warned the Israelites against idolatry worship that could easily attract the people of God. The Scripture revealed, "Son of man, these men have set up idols in their hearts and put wicked stumbling blocks before their faces. Should I let them insure of me at all? Therefore, speak to them and tell them, This is what the Sovereign Lord says: When any Israelite sets up idols in his heart and puts a wicked stumbling block before his face and then goes to a prophet, I the Lord will answer him myself in keeping with this great idolatry. I will do this to recapture the hearts of the people of Israel, who have all deserted me for their idols. Therefore say to the house of Israel, this is what the Sovereign Lord says: Repent! Turn from your idols and renounce all your detestable practices! When any Israelite or any alien living in Israel separates himself from me and sets up idols in his heart and puts a wicked stumbling block before his face and then goes to a prophet to inquire of me, I the Lord will answer him myself" (Ezekiel 14: 3-7).

God the Father in the Old Testament warned the people of Israel about worshiping idols. The elders of Israel were guilty of idolatry in their hearts; they were not loyal to God and His Word. The spurned God's will and desired an ungodly way of life; therefore, God refused to guide them by answering their prayers. In a similar manner, those today who look for guidance from God will find no help from His Spirit if their hearts are filled with ungodly desires for the sinfulness this of the world. In the New Testament Jesus Christ informed the Samaritan woman about false worship. According to the Scripture - Our Lord and Savior was speaking to the Samaritan woman at the well: "Yet a time is coming and has now come when the true worshiper will worship the Father in spirit and truth, for they are the kind of worshipers the Father seeks. God is a spirit, and his worshipers must worship in spirit and in truth" (John 4:23-24). Jesus Christ teaches several things in this scripture: "In spirit," He points to the level at which true worship occurs.

One must come to God in complete sincerity and with a spirit that is directed by the life and activity of the Holy Spirit. He stated that all true believing Christians worshipers must worship God the Father in Spirit and in truth which means the true worship of God takes place from inside our hearts, in the heart or from the spirit of worshipers which means the worship that is pleasing to God must be from a clean, transparent heart that is full of light offered with humble and purified hearts. "Praise the Lord, O my soul, all my inmost being ,praise his holy name. Praise the Lord, O my soul, and forget not all his benefits" (Psalm 103:1-2). The Psalmist expresses thanksgiving and praise to the Lord for all the benefits and blessings that He bestows on the believing covenant people.

We must never forget God's goodness to Christians believers. We must never forget to be faithful and thankful for God's blessings, in that He showered upon us through the Holy Spirit. We see also in the Scripture where it is very important to give thanks to God: "Has not my hand made all these things, and so they came into being declares the Lord. This is the one to esteem: he who is humble and contrite in spirit and trembles at my word" (Isaiah 66:2). God is impressed with the splendor of any building that humans construct for Him, but He does delight in a certain kind of person: those who are humble in spirit, who recognize their need for His continuing help and grace and who seek to follow His Word with all their heart. God will love dearly. God is telling us that this is where the worship in truth connects the heart, spirit of worship with the truth of God, and the work of God in redemption as well as revealed in Jesus Christ.

King David recognized the importance worshiping the Father in truth and the connection between the Word of God. The Scripture says, "Teach me your way, O Lord and I will walk in your truth, give me an undivided heart, that I may fear your name" (Psalm 86:11). "The Lord is near to all who call on him, to all who call on him in truth" (Psalm 145:18). All who call on God the Father in truth with a sincere and upright heart may be assured that He is near. He will hear their prayer, fulfill their desire for help and work for their deliverance. This is where the Old Covenant and the New Covenant connect. The true worship of God the Father is an essentially, specifically internal state; it is a matter of the heart by the power of the Holy Spirit who rooted the knowledge and obedience to the Word of God in the Scripture.

The Scripture warned from the Old Testament to the New Testament about religious hypocrisy and false gospel. We have seen how Elijah the prophet fought with the prophets of Baal by demonstrating the superiority of God of Israel's religion. Yahweh, also in the New Testament our Lord Jesus teaches about the issue with those who join faith and material things of this world together.

He told them that they cannot serve money or worship money and God at the same time. "No one can serve two masters. Either he will hate the one and love the other, or he will be devoted to the one and despise the other. You cannot serve both God and Money" (Matthew 6:24). Many people of this world serve money. They place money a high value on money. They place their trust and faith in money; they make money their ultimate security and happiness; they expect it to guarantee their future. People of this world desire money more than they desire God's righteousness and Kingdom. The danger of excessive accumulation of wealth is that it usually dominates people's mind and life, to the point that God's Kingdom and glory are no longer first in their lives.

Apostle Paul continuously condemned those who preach different gospels, perverted justification by faith in Christ and joining the teaching of Judaism and Christianity. "You foolish Galatians! Who has bewitched you? Before your very eyes Jesus Christ was clearly portrayed as crucified. I would like to learn just one thing from you: Did you receive the Spirit by observing the law, or by believing what you heard? Are you so foolish? After beginning with the Spirit, are you now trying to attain your goal by human efforts? Have you suffered so much for nothing if it really was for nothing?" (Galatians 3:1-4). It is only through faith in Jesus Christ we receive the Holy Spirit and all his blessings, including the gift of eternal life. The person who seeks to be justified by observing the law does not receive the Spirit and life, for the law cannot impart new life, or eternal life. Our Lord and

Savior clarifies that the true worshiper is the one that the Father seeks to worship Him. Scripture revealed: "Woe to you, teachers of the law and Pharisees, you hypocrites You shut the kingdom of heaven in men's faces. You yourselves do not enter, nor will you let those enter who are trying to. Woe to you, teachers of the law and Pharisees, you hypocrites! You build tombs for the prophets and decorate the graves of the righteous. And so upon you will come all the righteous blood that has been shed on earth, from all the blood of righteous Abel to the blood of Zechariah son of Berekiah, whom you murdered between the temple and the alter" (Matthew 23: 13, 29, 35). Jesus Christ's words in this Scripture is constituting His most severe denunciation, His Words were directed against religious leaders and teachers who had rejected at least a part of the revealed Word of God and replaced it with their own ideas and interpretations. In the Old Testament worship it is very important because of two main reasons: The Scriptures are part of the New Testament Christ Jesus believers which means that the Old Testament Scriptures lead to the New testament Scripture.

Our Lord Jesus Christ taught, healed, and preached in the synagogues of Palestine. It later became the synagogue of early Christian's missionary outreach. Jewish Christians constituted themselves within the local synagogue congregations for many years of Church history, until the Jew - Gentle divided into two groups. During the New Testament period, the synagogues stood as the temple equivalent to the religious institution in Judaism. The synagogue was considered a substitute for the Temple as the religious institution of Judaism. The influence on early Christian worship for the first century was that the Jewish Christianity began in the synagogue as a tradition with considerable impacts on the growth of the early Christian Church, especially in the Church architectural area of organization and the Lord's Supper. The Scripture revealed that the concept of elders in the synagogue was carried over into the early Church. The first deacons of the Christian church were charged with the same charge of the almoners of the ancient Jewish synagogue, gathering and distributing charitable gifts to the poor and needy believers (Acts 6: 1-7).

We have to know that the influence of the general principles of the Jewish synagogue worship of the early Church may be seen in the Church's commitment to prayer and reading of the Scriptures. Therefore, the worship of the early Christian church was founded upon praises, prayer, and the exposition of the Scriptures. Christian worship continues to develop in worshiping communities throughout the centuries of Church history. The form of Christian worship gradually changed and the Jewish worship especially when the Church began to grow, increasing the number of Gentiles. The truth we need to know is that the synagogues' worship in the early Church and the appreciation of Jewish roots of the Christian tradition. The Jewish roots of early Christianity which has grounded the Church of Jesus Christ solid belief of the divine and supernatural origin of the Bible, as well as the ordained apostolic authority in the divine authority of the Old Testament.

The way of worship by the early Church, the Jewish Christians of the first century, facilitated the shift from worship characteristic of Judaism to the Christocentric and Trinitarian worship, which is the main focus of Christianity. The Church inherited the concept of the centrality of the Scripture in worship from the Jewish synagogue, to include the giving of spiritual gifts according to the empowerment of the Holy Spirit in the life of believing Christians in churches today. The early Church was primarily encouraging the participation of worship by believers. The shift from Judaism to Jewish Christianity is not an easy task because of the dominating factors in the early Church Christianity. The Scripture revealed that one of the issues was ethnic and cultural diversity, which debated the implications of the Gospel of Jesus Christ for the Jew and Gentile can also be read in Acts 15:1-35. The compromise solution that was achieved at the first Jerusalem Council was in effective till today.

The Church also continues to debate on the relationship of law and grace in the life of all believing Christians. The relationship of Jesus Christ is the primary institutions of Judaism, the priesthood, the Temple and the sacrificial worship. The authority of the Scripture, interpretation, demonstrated that Jesus Christ as the Great High Priest, the more perfect temple and the ultimate sacrifice for sin of humanity. As a result many Jewish were unable to accept the teaching and the Scriptural interpretation of Jesus Christ, which abolished the first order of the Old covenant and other forms of practice of worship to establish a new order of practicing worship. "Then he said, 'Here I am, I have come to do your will.' He sets aside the first to establish the second," (Hebrews 10:9) which means the worship of continual praise and the worship of doing good. "Through Jesus, therefore, let us continually offer to God a sacrifice of praise - the fruit of lips that confess his name. And do not forget to do good and to share with others, for with such sacrifices God is pleased" (Hebrews 13: 15-16). The Gentile Church did not appreciate the Jewish roots of Christianity and it further compounded division between Jew and the Gentile. Today many Christian Churches are still struggling to implement Jew and the Gentile worship. "I am not ashamed of the gospel, because it is the power of God for the salvation of everyone who believes; first for the Jew, then for the Gentile. For in the gospel righteousness from God is revealed, a righteousness that is by faith from first to last, just as it is written: The righteous will live by faith" (Romans 1: 16-17). A righteous Christian believer will continue to live by faith, and in so doing he will grows from one level of maturity to another. In this way, the believer progresses along the path of righteousness to live a rich and full spiritual life with Christ Jesus.

In the New Testament worship we see clearly that outward obedience and religious practices, which required and approved are based on knowing Jesus Christ through sincere faith in Him, His redemptive work on the Cross, and love for Him, because of who Jesus Christ is; our mediator of a New Covenant. The Scripture revealed that in the Book of Deuteronomy speaks in chapter ten:

"And now, O Israel, what does the Lord your God ask of you but to fear the Lord your God, to walk in all his ways, to love him, to serve the Lord your God with all your heart and with all your soul," (Deuteronomy 10:12). God the Father Almighty has repeatedly emphasized the necessity of love that comes from the heart. God did not want His people to substitute passion and heartfelt love for Him with mere outward religious forms, such as keeping commandments, offering sacrifices, and the like, it was necessary that they always obey God from a heart that sincerely loved and honored Him. To the New Testament believers, faith and love from the heart are also essential to our relationship with God the Father. Yes, and it is indeed possible to read the Scripture, pray, attend church and partake of the Lord's Supper without a heartfelt devotion to God Himself; this is what is meant by legalism. Outward obedience and correct religious practices have a validity and significance only if they are based on knowing Jesus Christ through sincere faith in Him and love for Him because of who He is and what He has done for us.

All Churches Be One

"The Spirit of the Lord is on me, because he has anointed me to preach good news to the poor. He has sent me to proclaim freedom for the prisoners and recovery of sight for the blind, to release the oppressed, to proclaim the year of the Lord's favor" (Luke 4:18-19). The Scripture revealed the description of the Messiah and His anointing as related to the Messiah's mission or ministry which Jesus Christ Himself quoted in the Gospel of Luke. He quoted these verses and applied them to Himself in order to fulfill His ministry; Jesus Christ was anointed with the Holy Spirit.

Chapter Eleven

Catholic Churches' Doctrinal Ministry

Catholic Churches 606 AD- Boniface III was the first Pope, universal Bishop or Pope. In 1870 AD, the Vatican Council proclaimed that the Pope's decisions pertaining to the Catholic Church is infallible. One of the doctrines that is man-made is the original sin which they claimed that a newborn baby inherited from Adam and Even. According to the Bible Scripture we do not inherit sin, we commit sin, and we sin against God. The Scripture says - "Everyone who sins breaks the law, in fact, sin is lawlessness. But you know that he appeared so that he might take away our sins. And in him is no sin" (1st John 3:4-5). A newborn baby cannot commit sin. In order to clean the newborn baby from original sin they sprinkle water on him or her as a sign of baptism. "Peter, Repent and be baptized, every one of you, in the name of Jesus Christ for the forgiveness of your sins. And you will receive the gift of the Holy Spirit" (Acts 2:38). Repentance, for forgiveness of sins and baptism are the prior conditions for receiving the gift of the Holy Spirit. However, Apostle Peter's demand for his hearers on the day of Pentecost is that they should baptized in water before receiving the promise of the Father, must not be taken as an absolute requirement of the infilling with the Spirit, nor is baptism in the Spirit an automatic consequence of water baptism. In this situation, Peter required that water baptism prior to receiving the promise because, in the minds of his Jewish listeners, the rite of baptism was taken for granted as being involved in any conversion decision.

Catholic Churches adopted a doctrine that says an adult must study all the Catholic doctrine: Catechism, Rite of Christian Initiation of Adults. This could continue for many years with the celebration of Sacraments of Initiation, which Catholics celebrated on the Holy Week/Saturday before Easter.

The Council of Trent and the Lateran Council in 1215 AD gave priests the power to forgive sins; according to the Scripture, only Jesus Christ can forgive sin upon the unbelievers' repentance. This is a false doctrine and is man made it and is also a commandment of Mman made doctrine by the Catholic Church. Catholics pray to the blessed Mary Virgin Mary because Jesus gave her to all of us as our mother when he was hung on the Cross through the disciple John. The blessed virgin Mary was foreshadowed in the Old Testament to the New Testament because at the wedding in Canaan when they ran out of wine, his mother Mary approached Jesus when they ran out of wine; His mother, Mary, approached Jesus because they ran out of wine, but Jesus' time had not yet come, and His time came because He told them what to do. Because of that, the Catholic Church made Man made doctrine and decided to be asking Mary for their needs instead of asking Jesus, praying to Jesus instead of Mary; believing that Mary will take their request to Jesus Christ.

They felt that Mary, with her privileges, is able to obtain for them many graces. To others, they feel that they just asked Mary to pray for them just as the same they will ask anyone to pray for them. They feel also that Mary is cleaner than they are. In the year 1214 AD, the Catholic Churches added praying to Mary and a Rosary based prayer; this is a Roman Catholic segmented prayer of Man made doctrine.

Catholic Churches consisted of the American Catholic Church, the apostolic Catholic Orthodox Church, Eastern Rite Catholic, Catholic United Churches, Ecumenical Catholic Church, Mariavite Old Catholic Church, Province of North America, Old Catholic Churches, Polish National Catholic Churches, Reformed Catholic Church, Roman Catholic Church, Society of Saints Pius-X and United Catholic Church. It is really amazing to learn about different names of Catholic Churches because a non-Catholic will believe in non-Catholic Church rather than the Roman Catholic Church.

There are so many different kinds of Catholic Churches, but one Pope. Many Christians in the world profess their faith in one and the Only Holy Trinity God, and one Catholic Churches using one Apostolic Creed, which usually referred to as a religious idea to create universality of the churches. Catholic Churches are all over the nations of this world. Catholic Churches is a Church that holds dearly the bodies' people in their Church as universal throughout the years.

The Roman came to America through Christopher Columbus who discovered America. Catholic Churches cannot be broken due to their strong faith with the expression of Christians faith are in Roman Catholic Church. They belief that the Holy Spirit continuously works in the life of individual believers, developing and bringing faith to its richest and fullest of the heart of believers. The Church Fathers of the Catholic Church instruct and teach the faith of full believers to study and understand the Scripture in order to live a full Christian life. For more than a thousand years Catholic Church doctrine and devotion were established without changes, the history of the Catholic Church is basically the history of Christianity. In many countries Christian doctrine and ecclesiastical authority struggle with other Churches. Apostle Peter was the first Pope in Rome and he served from AD 540-604.

The Catholic Churche was founded in AD 66 when Apostle Peter was crucified upside down in Rome. Catholics believe that Peter is the first Pope. Therefore, they believe that the Pope is to be viewed as the ruling head of the Church of Jesus Christ on Earth. Boniface was the first Pope apart from Apostle Peter. Catholic Churches teache the Scripture, and they revealed the truth which were needed for people's sin for the salvation of the people in the world. Catholic scriptures include the Books of Canon for the Old Testament, including Deuterocanonical books, the Apocrypha and 27-books for the New Testament. They believe in one God, the creator of all the souls of human beings on Earth, the Lord and Savior of all and in the eternal Holy Trinity, as the Father, Son, and the Holy Spirit. Jesus Christ, the incarnate true Son of God, who was 100% human and 100% divine, conceived of the Holy Spirit and born of the Virgin Mary, crucified on the Cross who died and was buried for the sins of humanity in all the world.

He was raised to life again and ascended into Heaven; He will be coming back in glory and all eyes shall see Him; He is coming back to judge the quick and the dead. Christ died for all the people in the worlds' sins. He is the Lamb that was sacrificed for our sins. God the Father infuses His gift of grace in a supernatural way in Christ for those who believe in Jesus Christ and were baptized, maintained the gift of grace by doing works of love, receiving penance and the Eucharist. Catholic Churches believe that after death the soul of the faithful person goes straight to Heaven or, if it is imperfectly purified in this life, after purgatory. While the soul of the evil and wicked people at the time of death immediately go to the place of punishment in Hell. Catholic Churches believe that the Church is the body of Christ, established by Christ Jesus with the Bishop of Rome.

The Pope, who may at any time pronounce doctrine required of all the Catholic Church members, is the earthly head of Jesus Christ in Unity, to be one in Christ in a sacred holiness, all over the world. The Catholic Church goes back as far as the apostle's era of early Christianity. The Catholic Church believes that baptism of sinners remove and wash away the sinners original sin that means sins from the day the person was born as an infant.

They believe that the Eucharist, of bread and wine is changed into Jesus' body and blood. Catholic Churches doctrine believe that Mary was conceived by her mother was free of sin means immaculate. She remained a virgin perpetually and it was assumed, which means they are not sure, whether her body ascended to Heaven and they also believed that she is the mother of the Church, and considered an object of devotion, veneration, and she is to be worshiped. Catholic Churches are doctrinally conservative and diverse in their beliefs. Many members, including priests, accept some of the liberal, and pluralistic teaching of the Church which are contradictable to the teaching of Christianity and the early Church, as well as the teachings of the apostles.

>(1) There is nowhere in the Scripture, that the Word of Christ and the Word of God says Mary was conceived by her mother free from sin. Everyone that came to this world came with the sin of Adam and Eve, that is why God the Father sent His only Son to the world to redeem humanity from their sins. God the Father imputed the sin of everyone that comes to the world on Jesus Christ. Believers in Jesus Christ, give their Life

to Him; you are automatically cleansed from your sin through the atonement of the blood of Jesus Christ.

(2) Mary is not to be worshiped - only the Trinity - Father, Son and the Holy Spirit - one God is to be worshiped. Christ is the one that died, was crucified for the sin of the people in the world, not Mary. Mary is a messenger of God, that brought the Messiah into the world. I hope that this doctrine can be changed and corrected from the Catholic doctrine so that the Catholic Churches doctrine will be one with other doctrines that are Bible based doctrine. Mary did not bodily assume into Heaven. The Catholic Church must erase that word completely from their teaching of the Scripture. Blessed Mary, mother of Jesus Christ, died and was buried just as the apostles. She did not bodily ascend to Heaven. Assumed is a language that means not sure, once we are not sure of any particular incident, and it is not written in the Bible, we should not affirm it.

(3) In terms of the teaching of purgatory, it is impossible. A person either believes in Jesus Christ, or not from this earth. After death there is only two places either, Heaven or Hell. The soul must be perfect for Heaven from this Earth, there is no place the dead can stay for further purification. I strictly advise every individual

people on this Earth, to make sure that they live a life that is worthy of eternal life in Jesus Christ before they die. Jesus Christ will not take anyone half, half. You either know the Trinity and give your total life to Jesus Christ so that you can live with Him in heaven, or you don't, there is nowhere in the Scripture that says someone will stay for a soul's purification. If someone is saved, and falls into sin after being saved, the Spirit of the person will be saved, because once you gave your life to Christ, and He accepts you, He will not throw you out. Your spirit will always be saved into the hands of Jesus Christ. If this is what Catholic Churches definition of purgatory will take a whole book in order to analyze and explain; it is a different topic that will take a book by itself for the understanding of the Christian believers.

Roman Catholic Beliefs

Roman Catholic's beliefs and practices which are founded upon the first Vatican Council which was referred to as the, "Deposit of faith given to it by Christ and through his apostles, sustained by the Bible and by tradition." Catholic Churches strongly believe in Sacraments: (1) Baptism - necessary for membership in the Church, from infants and adults by pouring water or by immersion, as well as anointing with oil in the form of sign of the Holy Cross after baptism. (2) Confirmation is by laying of hands by a bishop but today priests can also confirm people or members (3) Eucharist, or Holy Communion - is the center of the Catholic devotion which is in the form of bread and wine – that means the body of Jesus Christ and the blood of Jesus Christ so that the worshiper or the congregation will be able to commune spiritually and physically with their Savior and Lord. (4) Sacrament of Reconciliation - also called Penance whereby, the sins are forgiven. (5) Anointing the sick, those who are seriously sick, or seriously injured and the Senior Citizens. (6) Sacrament of the Holy Orders which is for the ordination of deacons, priests, and bishops. (7) Sacrament of Marriage - which must not or cannot be dissolved by any human power whereby - remarriage after divorce and improper marriages may be annulled.

Catholic Churches' members are required to attend Mass on Sundays and on Holidays. They must fast, confess yearly their sin, receive the Holy Eucharist during the Easter, contribution to support the Church and observe the marriage rules and regulations of the Church. The central act of worship in Catholic Churches is Mass Liturgy of the Word and the Liturgy of Eucharist. They also use prayers using a Rosary, which means counting of beads on string as well as station of the Cross.

"Then he rolled up the scroll, gave it back to the attendant and sat down. The eyes of everyone in the synagogue were fastened on him, and he began by saying to them, "Today this scripture is fulfilled in your hearing." All spoke well of him and were amazed at the gracious words that came from his lips. Isn't this Joseph's son, they asked" (Luke 4:20-22). Jesus gives the purpose of His Spirit anointed ministry which is to preach the Gospel to the poor, the destitute, the afflicted, the humble, those who are crushed in spirit, the brokenhearted, and to heal diseases.

Chapter Twelve

Apostolic Catholic Orthodox Churches' Doctrinal Ministry

Apostolic Catholic Orthodox churches is the one of the largest old Catholic Churches. The standards are true to the Old Catholic where Eucharist is centered as the main doctrine of the Church; it does not discriminate against anyone because of their race, gender or marital status. People in the Church are open to marry, three major orders of worship where emphasized of the importance of loving local community that deals with the spiritual and social needs of the people in the world.

<u>Eastern Rite Catholic Churches</u> - The Eastern Catholic Churches hold a special position in the Roman Catholic Church. They are permitted to marry a clergy; they always service bread and wine. The eastern rite Churches are governed by the Vatican with the Eastern Rite Churches.

All Churches Be One

Ecumenical Catholic Churches - Ecumenical Catholic Churches is part of the Old Catholic movement, which defines itself as Catholic in doctrine and liturgy. They consider their Bishops to be the succession from Apostle Peter; their mission is a response to preach the Messianic Gospel of Liberation and Justice, offer refuge to those who are in Christ and suffer prejudice as well as confirm their life and teachings to the Lord Jesus Christ. They also promote the ordination of women and about 90% of their members are from Roman Catholic.

Mariavite Old Catholic Church - Mariavites are very different and are type of Old Catholic Church. Mariavites means "to imitate the life of Mary" the mother of Jesus Christ. Originated from Poland in 19th Century, in 1893 they respond to a vision. Their main goal is to maintain a deep spiritual life among themselves and their faithful pastors. They covenant to grow in members up till today.

Old Catholic Churches - They were English speaking Old Catholics who gathered together men of the Roman Catholic Monks.

Polish National Catholic Churches - Represented a different type of Old Catholic Church movement in Eastern Europe - Polish language and English are used in their worship services and in their educational programs of schools taught by pastors, clergy allowed to marry since 1921, but with the permission of the Bishops.

Reformed Catholic Church- Is one of the several bodies that were separated from the Roman Catholic Churches in order to promote greater openness to the modern world without denying their traditional Catholic worship; spiritually, sacrament and theology. Its rite is influenced by the Orthodox tradition, they still consider their priest to the in the Catholic Church.

Roman Catholic Churches - Roman Catholic Churches is the largest religious body of the Catholic Church. They claim their existence and beginning from the time that Jesus Christ appointed Apostle Peter as guardian of the keys to the gates of Heaven and Earth and as the Chief of the apostles. According to Roman Catholic teaching, Apostle Peter who was martyred in Rome during the time of Nero was the first Bishop of Rome and thus he was the first Pope. Roman Catholic offers one of the most significance, comprehensive and sophisticated theological teaching systems of religion which encourages a more intellectual and inquisitive approach to faith on the part of some people in the Church. Catholic Churches believe in faith and work, but faith alone in God for our salvation; not any work of our own can earn us salvation, it is the gift of grace of God to the salvation of soul of humanity. The structure of the Roman Catholic Church governing body is hierarchical - the head is the Pope who is the Bishop of Rome "vicar" of Christ on Earth and the visible head of the Church. The Pope's authority is supreme in all matters of faith and discipleship. Roman Catholic Churches have made a tremendous contribution to culture and society through its numerous and various as well as to catholic hospitals, education from elementary schools to the Universities; they made many charitable contribution through many organizations around the world. They remain strong and continuously growing in religious body of Christ all over the world. Roman Catholics are very concern about abortion, the right of the poor and the needy, caring for the sick and disabled people in the world.

<u>Society of Saint PiusX</u> - Society of Saints is a society of priests inside the Roman Catholic Church, it is not a separate denomination, and it is not recognized by Vatican. The focus of society of Saints PiusX is to promote the tradition of the Latin Mass and the decrees of the first Vatican Council through campaign.

<u>United Catholic Church</u> - The united Catholic Churches new organization of Catholic Churches grew out of the independent Catholic movement of the Old Catholic Churches. They rejected the Papal infallibility and seek to remain true to the Old Catholic Church teaching. They continue to line up with Vatican II with an emphasis on social justice, peace work, and inclusivity. It defines itself as ecumenical non-Judgmental and inclusive, it made a distinction between forgiveness and condoning sin. The Church was established and maintained moral traditional standards without legalistic and it promoted classic Catholic teaching of the early Church during the apostle's time. We can see clearly that within the Catholic Churches in the world there are diverse, and difference of opinion, beliefs and worship.

Grace D. Balogun

Christ in the Old Testament always intercedes for people of God and He is always with them. According to the Scripture, Christ is the guest who showed up at Abraham's Tent at Mamre. "The Lord appeared to Abraham near the great trees of Mamre; while he was sitting at the entrance of his tent in the heat of the day – Genesis 18:1, 6. He is the traveler who wrestled with Jacob until day break and Jacob said. "I will not let you go unless you bless me"(Genesis 32:22-31). Christ is the Commander of the Lord's Army who puzzled Joshua - Joshua 5:14-15. Christ is the fourth man who appeared in the fiery furnace with Shadrach, Meshach, and Abed-Nego – Daniel 3:25. Christ is the Angel of the Lord who appeared to Moses at the burning Bush - Exodus 3:1-15. Christ is the Melchezadez King of Salem who blessed Abram – Genesis 14:18-20. Christ became a human through the womb of the Virgin Mary. At His birth He became the God-Man fully God and fully man. – Luke 1:26-35, 2:7-14. It is a great comfort to know that Jesus Christ is always with His people, those who believe in His words, Christ said: And surely I am with you always, to the very end of the age" -Matthew 28: 20.
(Words of Grace Dola Balogun 2012)

Chapter Thirteen

Orthodox Churches' Doctrinal Ministry

Orthodox Churches believe in the Trinitarian God - the Incarnate of the Son of God, and the return of Christ to judge the quick and the dead. They also hold beliefs that Christ is fully man and fully God. Christ became fully human that people of this world might be able to have the energy of God's life in them. Also, through baptism and participation in the Church, God's people, the children of God, those who put their trust in Christ may receive the gift of Christ's redeeming work of redemption as they persevere in faith. Orthodox Churches believe that at death when one died, the souls of the faithful human being are purified as needed, a process of growth not punishment, then get a foretaste of eternal blessing in Heaven; while the souls of the wicked get a foretaste of eternal torment in Hell. Orthodox Churches believe that the Church is the body of Christ; Orthodox believe in the connection with the apostles, and changelessly maintained the faith of the Church as expressed in the Catholic Church Creeds means that one holy Catholic, and apostolic with Churches organized nationally by Armenian, Greek, Russian, with its Bishops under the leadership of the Pope being recognized as one of which Constantinople maintained primacy of honor. The Bishop initiates God's life on the one baptized, whether infants or adult. In the Eucharist, bread and wine are exchanged to the body and blood of Christ, which is a mystery that is unexplainable. The Orthodox Church also believes that Mary ascended bodily into Heaven, but they strongly believe images of Jesus Christ, many of the Saints are objects of veneration through which God is to be worshiped. The Orthodox significant proportion of their doctrine is conservative. Most Orthodox bodies are the members of the world council of Churches who's liberal cleanings have long caused a concern.

" He replied, The knowledge of the secrets of the kingdom of heaven has been given to you, but not to them.. Whoever has will be given more, and he will have an abundance. Whoever does not have, even what he has will be taken from him." (Matthew 13:11-12) Christ Jesus speaks these parables in order to alert his disciples to expect the presence or infiltration of evil with his visible kingdom, and to teach them how to overcome the influence and opposition of Satan and his followers.

Chapter Fourteen

Lutheran Churches' Doctrinal Ministry

The Lutheran Church was founded in 1517 by Martin Luther - when he challenged the Catholic teaching. This marked the beginning of the Protestant Reformation of the year 1530. Emphasis on the Lutheran confessional statements and the inerrancy of the Scripture, the Lutheran Church has given a great deal of attention to the ministry to the deaf, the disabled, the blind, and they produce series of literature in Braille and supported nearly sixty congregations who are hearing impaired. They continue to work with the world hunger relief and resettlement of refugees. They believe that Scripture alone is the authoritative witness to the Gospel where by some part of the Scripture are more directly or more fully than others. The Lutheran Church has more conservative view of Scripture as inerrant, thirty-nine Old Testament books and twenty-seven New Testament books were accepted. They believe in one Creator, Lord of all the people in the Universe. The Lutheran Church believes in eternally as the

Trinity: Father, Son, and Holy Spirit. And Christ as the Son incarnate, fully God and fully man conceived and born of the virgin Mary, that died on the Cross for the sins of humanity, rose bodily from the grave, ascended into Heaven, and will come back again to judge the people of the world. Lutheran Churches believe that we are saved by grace alone when God imputed to us His gift of righteousness through faith alone in Christ, who died for our sins. God's works are the result of true faith, but in no way the basis of our right standing before God. The Lutheran Church also holds the belief that the souls of Christian believers are, upon dying, go immediately to be with Christ their Lord and at Christ's return, their bodies are raised to immortal, or eternal life, the souls of the wicked suffer immediately in Hell. A Lutheran Church is the congregation of believers though mixed with the lost in which the Gospel is taught and the sacraments rightly administered. Lutheran's believe that all believers are priests in that they have direct access to God.

All ministers are pastors; and some serve as bishops. They rejected the apostolic succession of Pope. Lutheran Churches believe that baptism is necessary for believer's salvation, for both adults and infants are given the grace of God. Lutheran Churches believe in the Lord's Supper, which remains truly bread and wine, but which also becomes truly the body of Christ and the blood of Christ. Lutheran Churches liturgy is very similar to the Episcopal Church; they affirm that God chooses who will be saved before they believe. Lutheran Churches approve fully of the communion

Grace D. Balogun

with Episcopal Churches. The only difference in the Lutheran Church is the ordination of Gay and Lesbian as pastors, which churches have not been doing or approve of doing.

" He told them another parable: The kingdom of heaven is like a mustard seed, which a man took and planted in his field. Though it is the smallest of all your seeds, yet when it grows, it is the largest of garden plants and becomes a tree, so that the birds of the air come and perch in it braches" (Matthew 13:31-32).

Christian believers must be concerned about growing together in Christ's truth. One important point should be noted throughout the years of the Gospel before the return of Christ. God will not command His angels to destroy the children of the evil one until the end of the age.

Chapter Fifteen

Anglican Churches' Doctrinal Ministry

Anglican denominations were separated from Episcopal Churches in order to preserve the tradition, especially the 1928 prayer book. They offer Seven Sacraments to all the people of God with respect to the diversity of creation. The churches based its practice and doctrine on the idea of the original blessings in creation and they call to bring the message of salvation to all the people in the world. Anglican Churches hold beliefs that the Scripture is based on the truth, essential for salvation, and is primarily the norm for faith that must be interpreted in the light of the tradition and reason. They hold the belief in one Creator and the Lord of all existing, as the Trinitarian Father, Son, and the Holy Spirit. Further believing that Jesus Christ is the incarnate begotten Son of the Father, both human and divine, conceived of the Holy Spirit, born of the virgin Mary and whom died on the Cross for the sin of all human race in the universe; the third day He rose again from the grave, ascended into Heaven and will come again for the Church and to judge the quick and the dead and all eyes shall see Him. The Anglican Church believes that Christ suffered on the

Cross as an offering for sins and Christ freed us from sin, thus reconciled humanity to God the Father. Anglican Churches believe that we share in Christ's victory when in baptism we become living members of the Church, believing in Christ and keeping His commandments. Anglican Churches believe that the souls of faithful are purified as to enjoy full communion with God and at the return of Christ they are raised to the fullness of eternal life in Heaven.

Those who rejected God face eternal death. Anglican Churches believe that the Church is the body of Christ whose unity is based on the apostolic succession; they believe that bishops go back as far as the apostles, of whom the bishop of Rome is one of many; it is one Holy Apostolic. Anglican communion is a part of the Church, whose unity worldwide is represented by the archbishop of Canterbury Anglican Church is known in U. S. as Episcopal Churches. The same sacraments are the outward and visible signs of an inward and spiritual grace, infants and converts are made part of the Church in baptism. Christ's body and blood made part of present in communion members of Anglican are free to reject Catholic doctrines of Mary. The Book of Prayer is the norm for liturgy; priests may marry. The Episcopal Church approved the ordination of women also approved the ordination of gay bishops and also allowed bishops to bless same sex union. In the united States most Anglicans belongs to the Episcopal Church and are doctrinal conservative, such as the reformed Episcopal Churches and the Anglican Churches in North America. The only changes in Anglican Churches is the ordination of gay bishops and the blessing of the same sex union.

" I baptize you with water for repentance. But after me will come one who is more powerful than I, whose sandals I am not fit to carry. He will baptize you with the Holy Spirit and with fire" *(Matthew 3:11-12)*. John the Baptist was preaching and baptizing people for repentance, which will be accompanied by the fruit of righteousness. True saving faith and conversion must become evident through the lives that forsake sin and bear godly fruit.

Chapter Sixteen

Episcopal Churches' Doctrinal Ministry

The Episcopal Church is the largest body to come out of the Church of England. In the United States the church has been known as the Episcopal Church since 1967. Members of the Episcopal Church profess two of the ancient Christian Creeds: The Apostle's Creed and the Nicene Creed. Thirty-five articles were derived from the Church of England and thirty-nine articles were accepted as a general statement of the doctrine, both adherences to them as a Creed, which is not required.

At the ordination ceremony, the clergy will profess their belief in the Scripture and willingness to be able to conform to the doctrine, which are discipline and worship of the Episcopal Church. The Church expects its members to be loyal to the doctrine, discipline, worship of the one Holy Catholic and Apostolic Church in all the essentials. They permit great liberty in nonessentials. It allows for variation, individuality, independent, thinking and religious liberty. Some of the Episcopal Churches are more elaborate in ritual and ceremony, while others are very low with less stylized ceremony and more of an Evangelical's doctrine such as more emphasis on liberals, conservatives, modernists and evangelical which is a common ground for worship and prayer to include a deep sense of continuity in the Christian faith, spiritual and tradition. The Church sponsors eleven accredited seminaries; there are eight Episcopal Colleges and Universities in the United States and two Universities in abroad with over 1,100 Episcopal schools and early childhood educational programs that are in operation. Each Diocese sponsors several services and health organizations, including homes for Senior Citizens, youth care, hospitals and hospice centers. There are centers for the homeless and the poor, as well as destitute. The Episcopal Church in the United States organized over eleven Christian communities. After many trials and debate, the Church adopted a new standard of the Book of Common Prayer, which revised the American prayer book of 1928. The Liturgical Reform coincided with a vigorous pursuit of women's ordination to the priesthood that passed and approved in the General Convention in 1976.

In 2003 the church chose and ordained an openly gay individual as a Bishop and the blessing of same sex unions promises to be a difficult test for the Episcopal Church. Members remain focused primarily on the work of the ministry in parish communities. The Episcopal Church is more engaging in domestic evangelism that ever before. There are 90 million members in America.

Grace D. Balogun

The word of the Lord came to me, saying, "Before I formed you in the womb I knew you, before you were born I set you apart; I appointed you as a prophet to the nations" (Jeremiah 1:4-5.) God called Prophet Jeremiah to serve him during the time that the nation of Israel was rebelling against God and relying on political alliances to gain deliverance from its enemies. Prophet Jeremiah urged the people to repent of their sins and he warned them that they would indeed suffer punishment for rejecting God and his law.

Chapter Seventeen

Presbyterian Churches' Doctrinal Ministry

In 1536 John Calvin writes the institute of the Christian Religion – (1643-1649) - Westminster standards define Presbyterian doctrine - 1789. The Presbyterian Church of USA was established. They believe that the Scripture is the inspired and infallible and it is the sole final rule of faith. The Word of God witnesses, without doubt of Jesus Christ, but in merely human standards words reflecting beliefs of the time; the same standard that the Protestant accepted. The Presbyterian Church believes in one Creator and Lord of all, eternally as the Trinity: Father, Son and the Holy Spirit. They believe in the incarnate Son of God, fully divine and fully human, conceived and born of the Virgin Mary, who died on the Cross for the sin of the people in the world. That He rose in a bodily form from the grave, ascended into Heaven and that He will be coming back in His glory to judge the quick and the dead and all eyes shall see Him. Presbyterian Churches teach, by their doctrine, that they were saved by grace alone when God the Father imputes to humans His gift of righteousness through faith alone in Christ, who died on the Cross and rose again for our sins.

People maintain good works through, and as a result of the believer's faith, but not on the basis of our on righteousness before God. They believe that the souls of believers upon dying go immediately to live with Jesus Christ. When Christ returns, the bodies of the believers will be raised to immortal, eternal life and the souls of the wicked begin suffering immediately in Hell after death. Presbyterian Churches teach that the Church is the body of Christ, including the people that God has chosen as His people, which is represented by the visible Church, composed of churches that vary in purity and corruption.

Christ alone is the Head of the Church. The elders of the church are chosen by the congregational members. Presbyterian Churches believe that baptism is not necessary for salvation, but it is a sign of the New Covenant of grace for adult and infants. Jesus' body and blood are spiritually present to believers in the Lord's Supper. The five points of Calvinism were affirm: Humans are so sinful that they cannot initiate return to God, God chooses who will be saved; Christ died specifically to save those whom God chose; and infallibly draws to Christ those whom He chooses; they will never fall away. The Presbyterian Church is the largest doctrinally conservative church.

I disagree with one or two of their doctrine: which says Christ come only to save the elect. Jesus Christ Himself said in the Scripture that there is no one that comes to Him, will be sent away.

Yes, the elect of God will be saved, but Christ came for the people of the whole world, for forgiveness of their sins, resurrection and eternal life. God the Father makes people, sinners alive in Him; He imparted the life of Christ into unbelievers so that He can save them from their sin. The Presbyterian Church believes that baptism is not necessary for salvation - They rule out the Word of the Lord that says, "Go ye and make the disciples of all nations baptizing them in name of the Father, Son, and Holy Spirit." What they were saying in their Christian doctrine is that they don't have to carry out the commandment of the Lord Jesus Christ, if Baptism is not necessary for salvation; our Lord will not order the disciple, the apostle to baptized even our Lord Himself were baptized by John the Baptist in River Jordan. God the Father acknowledge His baptism when He said from Heaven, " This is my beloved Son in whom I am well pleased." At the same time the Dove descended from Heaven unto Jesus Christ. I pray that the Presbyterian Church make a correction of this error in their doctrine so that people will be saved and fully complete in Christ.

"But you, Bethlehem, in the land of Judah, are by no means least among the rulers of Judah; for out of you will come a ruler who will be the shepherd of my people Israel" (Matthew 2:6. King Herod attempted to kill Jesus and God's way of protecting the child reveal several truths about God's method of guiding and protecting His people. God did not protect Joseph and Mary and Baby Jesus without their cooperation. Protection requires obedience to God's guidance, which in this case involved fleeing the country.

All Churches Be One

Chapter Eighteen

Protestant Reformed Churches' Doctrinal Ministry

The Protestant Reformation was the Schism within Western Christianity, initiated by Martin Luther, John Calvin and other Protestants. There are so many people that wanted to change, but they were unable until Martin Luther made a significant attempt and reform started. Reformation began in 1517 when Luther published his Ninety Five Thesis. It also influences the Church of England after 1547. The separation of the Church of England - Anglican Church from Rome under Henry VIII, beginning in 1529 and was completed, and ended in 1537, which brought the Anglican Church - alongside the broad reformation movement.

In 1924 three pastors of the classic Grand Rapids from the East and from the West of the Christian Reformed Church in North America were deposed from the denomination as a result of disagreement over the doctrine of common grace. This doctrine states that grace is extended in some measure to those who are not part of God's elect. Herman Hoeksema (1886-1965) was foremost among those who taught that grace for the elect alone is an essential aspect of the Reformed faith.

Many people within the congregation were objected to the doctrine and they were forced out of the Church, which was formally organized as the Protestant Reformed Churches in America in 1926. The Church holds three basic Reformed Confessions. The Heidelberg Catechism of 1563, The Belgic Confession of 1561, and the Canon of Dort of 1618 as the basis of their belief in the infallible Word of God. In the government they are Presbyterian, they have two classes of geographical organized body membership in the upper West. The Church maintained a Theological Seminary in Michigan.

The Protestant Reformed Church in America is a denomination of thrirty-one churches and has over 7,800 members. Their origin as a denomination was based on doctrinal controversy over common grace within the Christian Church. There are three points of common grace those who prove the common grace were suspended and some were deposed from office. The first point concerns God's favor towards His people, the people of this world not only the elect. They believe that apart from the saving grace of God to those who are the elect of God that God also stretched His favor, and grace to all His creatures in the universe. The Second point based on concerned with the restraint sin, and in the life of the individual sinners in the communities, that there is such a restraint of sin according to the Scripture and the confession, that God by the general operation of His Spirit, can restrain the unimpeded sin by which humanity's life will remain possible. Third point confession of unregeneration, which says that God without renewing the heart, will influence man that He is able to perform civil good. They believe that in obedience to the command of Christ, the Head of the Church they must preach the Gospel to all creatures as a duty and as a privilege of the Church to carry out their calling.

They were very active in missions domestically and in about. They established Christian Schools from grade schools to high school. Protestant reformed Church have their beginning since 1924 and traces their spiritual doctrine as far back as to the apostolic era; early churches whose doctrine is the foundation of the Christian Church with Jesus Christ the Savior. They believe there is only one spiritual being God, He is the God of all perfection - God is known through His creations and preservation through the world. God also made Himself know through as the God of grace in Jesus Christ and in the His Holy Word, the Scripture - which reveals all what God wants us to know concerning salvation.

Grace D. Balogun

"And I will put my Spirit in you and move you to follow my decrees and be careful to keep my laws. You will live in the land I gave your forefathers; you will be my people, and I will be your God (Ezekiel 36:27-28). God promises to restore Israel not only physically, but also spiritually; this restoration involves giving them a new heart that is as tender as flesh so that they will respond to God's Word.

Chapter Nineteen

Presbyterian Churches' Doctrinal Ministry

The Orthodox Presbyterian Churches begins with a protest against the beliefs of modernistic practices by the Presbyterian Church. They laid strong emphasis on the infallibility and inerrancy of the Scripture. They believed that the writers of the Bible were guided and control by the power of the Holy Spirit, as well as by God the Father and God the Son. They believed that there is no error, also that the fundamental doctrines which includes the original sin, the virgin birth, the deity of Christ, His substitutionary atonement of Christ, His resurrection and His ascension, Christ's role as the Judge of the universe at the end of age; the consummation of the kingdom, the sovereignty of God, the salvation through the Lamb sacrifice and the power of Jesus Christ for those who are saved through the gift of grace by God the Father. Most importantly, they believe in the Trinity.

Grace D. Balogun

Korean - American Presbyterian Churches

The Korean American Presbyterian Church was established by the Korean immigrants in North America, founded in 1976. It is the largest Korean Christian Church in America; it is theologically conservative and observes Creeds that emphasizes the biblical inerrancy, the absoluteness of God, the sin of Adam and Eve; necessity of faith, works and obedience to the Law of God which is from saving faith.

Presbyterian Churches in America

The Presbyterian Church are the congregations that had withdrawn from Southern Presbyterian Churches. They opposed to the ecumenical inadvertent in the National Council of the Churches of Christ, the world Council of Churches; the consultation on Churches Union. They opposed the impending merger with United Presbyterian Churches of U.S. They also rejected the ordination of women. The Church teaches that the Holy Spirit guided the writers of the Scriptures so that there will be no error. They also emphasized on the doctrine of human depravity, salvation by grace Christ's death for the elect alone, perseverance of the Saints. They have a distinction between classes of elders: teaching elder - ministers and ruling elders means laymen. The only thing that is wrong in their doctrine is that they believe that Christ's death is for the elect alone. This doctrine is totally wrong, its needs to be corrected. Christ Jesus came to the world for all the people in the world; all the sinners in the world, and His death are for the sinners in the world as well as His bodily resurrection are for all the people in the world.

Presbyterian 1789 Church of USA

There are two of the largest Presbyterian Churches both of them were reunited in 1983 - Great efforts were made in order to combine the two Churches together - Southern Churches has been established since the civil war, and they were parallel, to the Northern Churches. They were Christ centered Church - they stress the concept of love one another, love for God, sin, external life, and the work of reconciliation in God, Christ and His Church. The book of confession with nine creeds was accepted by both churches.

Grace D. Balogun

"The word of the Lord came to me: son of man, take a stick of wood and write on it, Belonging to Judah and the Israelites associated with him. Then take another stick of wood, and write on it, Ephraim's stick, belonging to Joseph and all the house of Israel associated with him. Join them together into one stick so that they will become one in your hand" (Ezekiel 37: 15-17). God's people were divided into two kingdoms after King Solomon's death. One was called Judah and one was called Ephraim; God now promises that the two kingdoms will be reunited as one kingdom, with one King to rule over them.

Chapter Twenty

Methodist Churches' Doctrinal Ministry

Methodist Churches consisted of African Methodist Episcopal Church, African Methodist Episcopal Zion Church, Christian Methodist Episcopal Church, Congregational Methodist Church, Evangelical Church of North America, Korean Methodist Church, Primitive Methodist Church USA, Salvation Army, Southern Methodist Church, united Methodist Church, Volunteers of America, Inc., and Windsor Village United Methodist Church. Beginning from the Church of England in the year 1730, Methodist Churches expanded during the 17th Century under the leadership of John Wesley (1703-91) and Charles Wesley (1707-88); both of them preached of the Word of God and they are also song writers. The Methodist Church is more concerned for the poor, the under privileged and the disabled people of their time. They expressed their faith more in compassion for the suffering in various ways. Methodist Churches believe in the power of the Holy Spirit, love your neighbor and evangelization. The Methodist

Grace D. Balogun

Churches came to life through the group of small students at Oxford University because of their devotion to prayer, fasting, Bible reading and charitable works. Among the group were the Wesley's as well as George Whitefield (1714-70). Three of them were ordained the same day in the Church of England. Methodist Churches in the United States were born in 1769 in New York, which is now John Street Methodist Church. All other Methodist Churches follow after that their beliefs and practices. The Methodist Churches have stressed the fundamental beliefs and they have offered a common ground theological teaching - mentioning the doctrine of free will of the individual and the death of Jesus Christ as the atonement for human beings. The Church preaches and teaches the doctrine of the Trinity, the sinfulness of human beings, falling into sin and in need of repentance and conversion, freedom of will, justification by faith alone, sanctification and holiness that include future reward or punishments, the Word of the Bible, salvation, the grace of God, two sacraments, baptism, and communion.

In 1738, John and Charles Wesley were already devoted Anglican Ministers with the Great Awakening in 1784 in the USA. The Methodist Church formed a separate church. The doctrine is that Scripture is an inspired and infallible, the sole final rule of faith. The Scripture is the primary source and criterion for Christian doctrine, and may not be fallible. For most people this is the standard of the Methodist Church and the canon is accepted. They believe in one Creator and the Lord of all who is existing eternally as the Trinity: Father, Son, and the Holy Spirit. They teach about Jesus Christ as the incarnate, fully human and fully divine, conceived and born of the Virgin Mary, Christ's ascension into Heaven and that He will come back again to judge the people of the world. Methodist Church doctrine teaches that we are saved by grace alone when God regenerates and forgive us through our faith in Jesus Christ, who died for our sins. The Methodist Church doctrine says: Good works are necessary and is the result of believers' true faith in Christ, but it does not obtain forgiveness or salvation. They believe that the souls of believers upon dying go immediately to be with Jesus Christ and at Christ's return, their bodies will be raised to immortal eternal life. The wicked will suffer eternal punishment in Hell. Methodist Churches' doctrine teaches that the Church is the body of Jesus Christ, represented by visible Church institutions - Bishops oversee regions, appointing pastors, clergy and laity which meet together in a national conference every four years.

Baptism is a sign of regeneration and of the New Covenant and is for adults and children. Jesus Christ is always present to believers in the Lord's Supper. Methodist doctrine teaches that the sanctification is a work of the Holy Spirit subsequent to regeneration by which fully consecrated believers are purified of all their sins and are fit to serve the Lord. Believer's state maintained by faith and obedience. Worship and liturgy are based on the English Prayer book. African Methodist Episcopal Churches are one of the oldest and largest Methodist bodies in the

Grace D. Balogun

world. It was founded by Richard Allen (1760-1831), a former slave from Delaware who had bought his own freedom. Allen was converted when he was still a slave. He began preaching to free African- Americans in Philadelphia five times a day. Other African American churches throughout the Urban North follow suit.

"The hand of the Lord was upon me, and he brought me out by the Spirit of the Lord and set me in the middle of a valley; it was full of bones. He led me back and forth among them, and I saw a great many bones on the floor of the valley, bones that were very dry. He asked me, son of man, can these bones live?" (Ezekiel 37:1-3) By the power of the indwelling of the Holy Spirit, Prophet Ezekiel was taken to a valley full of bones. These bones represent the whole House of Israel whose hopes were lost and died when they were dispersed to exile to live among the foreigners who worship idols and other gods.

Chapter Twenty-One

Anabaptist Churches' and Mennonite

Anabaptist Churches and Mennonite consists of Beachy Amish Mennonite Churches, Bruder of Communities, Church of God in Christ, Mennonite, Conservative Mennonite Conference, Fellowship of Evangelical Mennonite Churches, General Conference of Mennonite, Brethren Churches, Hutterian Brethren, Mennonite Churches USA, Missionary Church, Old Order Amish Churches, Old Order Wisler Mennonite Church founded by Mennosimons, formerly a Roman Catholic Priest who was baptized by an Anabaptist Preacher in Holland in 1632. Their doctrines are as follows: faith in God the Creator, humanity's fall and restoration of coming of Jesus Christ, Christ is the Son of God, who redeemed human kind on the Cross, obedience to Christ's Law in the Gospel, the necessity of repentance and conversion for salvation; baptism as a public testimony of faith; the Lord's Supper as an expression of common union and fellowship. Most viewed the Scripture as the inspired means for knowing and following

Jesus, but not as infallible. Jesus is the Living Word. Scripture is the written Word that points to Him. The Standard of Protestant Canon is accepted. How believers live is emphasized over having correct doctrine. God is one Creator and Lord of all, revealed in Jesus Christ through the Holy Spirit. Most affirm the Trinity in some way; the doctrine says: The Savior of the world, a man in whom God's love and will are revealed by His life of service and His suffering and death. His deity, virgin birth, and resurrection are traditionally affirmed. Also, salvation is a personal experience in which, through faith in Jesus, we became at peace with God, moving us to follow Jesus' example as His disciples by living as peacemakers in the world.

Anabaptist Churches doctrine teaches that there is no official view of what happens immediately after death. At Christ's return God's people will be raised to eternal life and the unrepentant will be forever separated from God. They believe that the Church is the body of Christ, the assembly and society of Christ's disciples who follow Him in the power of the Spirit. It is to be marked by holiness, love, service and a church government is recognized; Leadership is to be characterized by humble service and is primarily, but not exclusively local. They believe that baptism is for believers only as a sign of commitment to follow Jesus. The Lord's Supper is a memorial of His death. Most Quakers view sacraments as spiritual only, not external rites. Anabaptist and similar bodies are peace directed churches, teaching nonresistance and pacifism, the view that all participation in war is wrong, doctrine is emphasized, and liberal views with social emphasis prevail in some church bodies including, most Quaker Churches. The Mennonite Church and Churches of the Brethren are the largest bodies, the Amish are a variety of Mennonite Quaker friends that originated separately, but share much is common with Anabaptist.

I disagree with Anabaptist doctrine that says: There is no view, or clue of what happens immediately after death. While it was in the Scripture clearly that those who did not believe in Jesus Christ, repent of their sin will go the eternal damnation, which is Hell. They should please correct this statement out of their doctrine so that their congregation will take sin seriously and be complete in Jesus Christ.

" I said, 'O sovereign Lord, you alone know'. Then he said to me, 'Prophesy to these bones and say to them, 'Dry bones, hear the word of the Lord! This is what the Sovereign Lord says to these bones: I will make breath enter you, and you will come to life' " (Ezekiel 37:3b-5). The bones were then raised to life in to stages; one as a political restoration to the land and the second one, as a spiritual restoration of faith. This vision was give to Ezekiel to assure the exiles that they would be restored by God's power and again become a living community in the Promised Land in spite of their seemingly hopeless circumstances they were going through at the present time.

Chapter Twenty-Two

Congregational Churches' Doctrinal Ministry

Congregational Churches have been established since 1607 as a house Church in London England. In 1620, congregational Churches move to Plymouth, Massachusetts, which they are still there today. The view of their doctrine is the Scripture as the authoritative witness to the Word of God that was living in Jesus, rather than viewing Scripture as the unerring Word of God. The Bible and Creeds are the testimonial of faith not test of faith. The Standard Protestant cannon is accepted. They believe that the eternal Spirit who calls the worlds into being and is made known in the man Jesus. The crucified and risen Savior and Lord, in whom we are reconciled to God. His deity and virgin birth are widely ignored or rejected, except in the conservative church bodies. God promises forgiveness and grace to save people from sin and aimlessness; all who trust Him, who accept His call to serve the whole human family. They believe that those who trust in God and live as Jesus' Disciples are promised eternal life in God's Kingdom.

No position is taken on the future of the wicked. Most reject the idea of eternal punishment. The doctrinal of the congregational holiness church affirms that basics of evangelical and Pentecostal, doctrines along with the idea of rapture of the Church, with the Second Coming of Jesus Christ, speaking in tongues which means the initial evidence of the experience of baptism in the Holy Spirit. They further believe in baptism by immersion, the Lord's Supper, and foot-washing. The doctrine of the congregational church is not clean. Those who trust in God and live as Jesus followers, the Church is the people of God living as Jesus' disciples by serving humanity as agents of God's reconciliation and love; each local church is self-governing and chooses its own ministers. The congregation may practice infant baptism or believer's baptism, or both sacraments are symbols of spiritual realities.

The United Church of Christ ordains various groups of people, both men and women to their ministry. The doctrine is not well structured and it is too liberal as to what the congregation can do or cannot do. They need to restructure their doctrine so that people will be more biblical as to what the doctrine is teaching the members and the people of the world.

Grace D. Balogun

"I will attach tendons to you and make flesh come upon you and cover you with skin; I will put breath in you, and you will come to life. Then you will know that I am the Lord" (Ezekiel 37:6.) We should see Israel's restoration to life to remind us of the creation of man in the Scripture in the Book of Genesis. Adam was first formed physically, after which God gave him the breath of life. In the same way Israel would be first restored physically and then God would give his breath of life by pouring out His Spirit on them.

Chapter Twenty-Three

Baptist Churches' Doctrinal Ministry

Baptists are Christian people who comprise of a group of denominations and churches that adopted the doctrine that says baptism should be performed for professing members salvation through faith alone and by Scripture alone to be their rule of faith and their practices. Baptists recognize two ministerial offices: pastors and deacons. Baptists today differ widely from one another in their beliefs. Some Baptist churches reject the baptism of infants by immersion, but recognize the adult baptism by immersion.

Baptist members are more than 41 Million - 150,000 congregations; 33 million in North America, 100 Million worldwide. In 1612 Tomas Helwys established a Baptist Congregation in London consisting of congregants from Smyth's Church – A member of Baptist Church was opened and they were called general Baptists.

Grace D. Balogun

Baptists, like other Christians churches, were defined by their doctrine - some of their doctrine were common to all Orthodox Churches and Evangelical groups and some of their doctrines are distinctive. Most Baptist churches are evangelical in doctrine. Baptists beliefs can vary due to the congregational governing system that gives individual local Baptist church autonomy. Baptists have played an important and encouraging role in religious freedom and in the Separation of Church and State. Baptist shared doctrine is that they believe in one God – the dead will be raised, and Christ will judge in righteousness.

John Smyth and other English Puritans form the first Baptist Church – 1639, the first Baptist Church in America was established. We also have Baptist Bible Fellowship International, Baptist Missionary Association of America, American Baptist Publication Society of American, Baptist convention, Cooperative Baptist Fellowship, Conservative Baptist Association of America, General Association of General Baptist Churches, Duck River Association of Baptists and the General Association of Regular Baptist Churches. The churches are comprised of one of the largest and most diverse of Christians in United States.

Scripture is inspired and it is without error, final, totally trustworthy. The rule of faith and the Standard Protestant canon is accepted and they continue to view Scripture as without error. They believe in the Eternal Son incarnate, fully God and fully human, conceived and born of the virgin Mary, died on the Cross for the sins of humanity, rose bodily from the grave, ascended into

Heaven, and will come again in His glory to judge humanity. The Baptist churches' doctrine stated and teaches that they are saved by grace alone when God imputes to us His gift of righteousness through faith alone in Christ, who died for our sins. God's work is a result of true faith, but it does not have any way for the basis of our right standing before God Almighty. The Baptist church teaches that the souls of believers upon dying go immediately to be with the Lord Jesus Christ; and at the return of Christ, the bodies of the believers will be raised to immortal, eternal life. The wicked will suffer eternal punishment in Hell.

They believe that the Church is the body of Christ, which consists of the redeemed throughout history. Churches usually and always refers to local congregations, each of which is members are baptized believers and whole officers are pastors and deacons. Churches may form associations or conventions for cooperative purposes, especially missions and education. Baptists believe in the immersion of believers, only as symbol memorial of Christ's death and anticipation of His return. Many Baptist churches emphasized evangelism and missionary work.

They also believe in separation of Church and state. Baptists Churches include Calvinists - Southern Baptist convention and Armenians - Free Will Baptist Church bodies. Largest Protestant Churches - American Baptists and National Baptist Churches. Baptists exercise freedom of thought and expression in the pulpit and pew. They insist on autonomy of the local congregation; every church arranges it own worship and form of baptism for its members. No age for membership, but they all must accept the teaching of Christ. Baptist Churches are bound together with strong principles and doctrines, which was based primarily on faith. They believe strongly on the inspiration and trustworthiness of the Scripture as the only rule of life in the Lordship of Jesus Christ; freedom to approach God directly through faith and the grace of God with the help of the Holy Spirit, the Lord's Supper, life after death, the unity of humanity, the law and commandment of God, the redemptive work of Jesus Christ from our sin, the establishment of God's freedom upon Christ's return.

Some Baptists believe that Baptist churches existed since the days of John the Baptist. The black Baptist Church preachers are very effective in converting African Americans to Christianity before the emancipation, and in pre-civil war days. Slaves usually set in the galleries of the churches identifying with their owners faith. Occasionally a black preacher might be liberated so that He will be able to give full time to God's work and Scripture among the black slaves. The first black Baptist Church was established in 1773. They were very concerned in foreign missions. Some Baptist churches believe that Jesus Christ died for the people in the world, instead for only the elect.

"So I prophesied as I was commanded. And as I was prophesying, there was a noise, a rattling sound, and the bones came together, bone to bone. I looked, and tendons and flesh appeared on them and skin covered them, but there was no breath in them" (Ezekiel 37:7-8). God's promise to restore any human being never fails. He is in control, and he has the power in Heaven and on Earth to do so.

Chapter Twenty-Four

Church of Christ Doctrinal Ministry

Churches of Christ were established in the year 1832 by Thomas and Alexander Campbell. They are servants of Jesus Christ. According to their teaching and doctrine they believe that, "Where the Scriptures speak, they speak and where the Scripture are silent they will be silent." Churches of Christ believe that Scripture is the inerrant Word of God; Jesus Christ's disciples are the witness too.

The Church of Christ's belief in the fallibility of Jesus Christ; standard cannon is accepted. The Standard canon is accepted. The one Creator is Lord of all. They rejected the creeds, but most of them accepted the Trinity of God Father, Son and Holy Spirit. They believe that the Son of God is fully God and fully human, conceived by the Holy Spirit, born of the virgin Mary, died on the Cross for our sins, rose bodily from the grave, ascended into Heaven, and will come again to judge all humanity. Churches of Christ believe that everyone must hear the Gospel, believe in Jesus

Christ, and they must repent from their sins, confessing Jesus Christ as Lord and Savior, be baptized, and persevere in holiness in order to be saved.

Churches of Christ believe that God saves human beings by His grace, when they respond by faith, believers immediately go to be with Christ and at His return they will be raised to immortality; the wicked will suffer eternally in Hell. Churches of Christ are the assembly of those who have responded rightly to the Gospel of God; it must be called by Christ's name only. And they are the only part of the restoration of true Christianity. Individual local churches are autonomous and call their own pastors, which they believe it is different from Disciples of Christ. The church's government that are ecumenical and did not claim the restoration of true Christianity. Baptism by immersion on believers only, as the initial act of obedience to the Gospel. Many Churches of Christ recognize baptism in their own churches only as the valid Baptism. They believe that the Lord's Supper is a symbolic memorial for Christians. Many, but not all Churches of Christ, forbid the using of any instrument of music of worship. International Churches of Christ teach that its members are saved and are widely reported to strongly influence its members.

The Churches of Christ are very wrong in their doctrine and teaching because we are saved by faith alone in Christ alone; they cannot say that their congregation of twelve thousand will fill the new earth when Christ returns to set up His Kingdom. They are to go and review the Scripture again from the Old Testament to the

New Testament and correct this gruesome error. Churches of Christ doctrine members of one Godhead strongly emphasis on the Church as the body and bride of Jesus Christ based on the Book of Revelation. Faith is in Jesus Christ the only begotten Son of the Father. Churches of Christ believe that final judgment of all religious groups is for the Lord to decide. They rejected any form of instrumental music; they used only a Cappella singing in worship. Missionary program is ongoing in over 92-nations outside the U.S. There are also international Churches of Christ, which emerge from the Restorationist movement; many of its former members are expected to confess their sins, which are recorded for future reference. Members are strictly instructed in Scriptures, teach that believer's baptism by immersion is necessary for salvation and for those who do not baptize are considered damned, and members must stay away from them. All members must devote their time to evangelize and the discipleship of the new members. My question is how are they going to evangelize if they stay away from those who are not baptized?

"Then He said to me, Prophesy to the breath; prophesy, son of man, and say to it. This is what the Sovereign Lord says: Come from the four winds O breath, and breathe into these slain, that they may live so I prophesied as he commanded me, and breath entered them; they came to life and stood up on their feet a vast army" (Ezekiel 37:9-10.) Ezekiel's vision of the dry bones would be fulfilled at the time of Israel's restoration, not only physically but also spiritually. This restoration was initially fulfilled during Ezekiel's time, but it will be fully realized when God gathers the Israelites to their land in the end time and a great spiritual awakening will occur. Many Jews will believe in the Gospel and accept Jesus Christ as their Messiah before He returns to establish His Kingdom.

Chapter Twenty-Five

Seven Day Adventists

The Seven Day Adventist group branched from one of the smaller Adventist groups. They believed that an event to place which is a significant event in 1844, the prophesied, an event in heaven itself. Christ's ministry in heaven moved from the Holy to the most Holy place. They understood this Holy Place as Christ's ministry of judgment according to the Book of Revelation. They believed that three group of Angelic Host revealed messages and focused on God's commandments and faith in Jesus Christ, seeking to show the relationship between the Old Testament and the New Testament gospel. They believe that all the faithful must observe the Ten Commandments in order to honor the seventh day of the biblical Sabbath. Therefore, this group of Adventist began to observe the Sabbath on the Seventh Day.

The Seven Day Adventist Churches believed that the observation of the Sabbath was to be away to await the advent of the Lord; therefore, they named it Seven Day Adventist. Seventh

Day Adventist consider the human body to be the temple of the Holy Spirit because of this revelation they abstain from alcoholic beverages, tobacco, and drugs. They advocate sound principles of healthful living through diet, exercise and Philanthropic outlook. Seventh Day Adventist teach and doctrinally, they are considered evangelical conservatives, holding to the authoritative Word of God through the inspiring of the written Scriptures. Seventh Day Adventist believe in the divine creation of humanity through Adam and Eve. They believe in Christ and that He will return to create a new earth; the time is unknown. They also believe in baptism of adult by immersion, practice feet washing in preparation for the Holy Communion. They also promote religious liberty and separation of the Church and State. They give generously and support the missions, and other churches' enterprise. Scripture is inspired and without error, totally trustworthy, is the rule of faith.

An early Seventh Day Adventist Leader was a prophet. Her writing continues to be the authoritative source of truth. One creator God, Unity of three co-eternal persons: the Father, Son, and Holy Spirit. Seventh Day Adventist's teach the eternal Son incarnate, fully human and fully divine, conceived of the Holy Spirit, born of the virgin Mary, died on the Cross for our sins, rose bodily from the grave, ascended into Heaven and He will be coming back go judge all the people in the world. Seventh Day Adventist's teach that to be saved, we must repent, believe in Jesus Christ in His life, death, and resurrection.

Grace D. Balogun

By grace we are made right with God and were sanctified as well as empowered by the Spirit to live in obedience to God's commandment those who are found to be obedient at the end will be saved. They teach that death of all people is an unconscious state. At Jesus Christ's return the righteous will be raised for life in Heaven. After a Millennium, the wicked will be raised only to be annihilated, the righteous will live forever on a new earth. Seventh-Day- Adventist's doctrine say the universal Church includes all who believe in Christ. The Last Days are a time of Apostasy during which a remnant keeps God's commandment faithfully. Baptism is by immersion and is contingent upon affirmation both of faith in Jesus Christ and Adventist doctrines. Baptism is to the Seventh Day Adventist Church. The Lord's Supper is a symbolic memorial of Christ's death is practiced quarterly every 3 months and follows by foot washing of the congregation. Rest and worship on Saturday is an essential element of obedience for all the Seventh Day Adventist believing Christians.

"This is the word that came to Jeremiah from the Lord: Go down to the potter's house, and there I will give you my message. So I went down to the potter's house, and I saw him working at the wheel. But the pot he was shaping from the clay was marred in his hands; so the potter formed it into another pot, shaping it as seemed best to him" (Jeremiah 18:1-4). Prophet Jeremiah was told to go to a potter's house, where he watched a potter fashioning a pot from clay. Because the vessel was not suitable for what the potter intended, he had to remold it into something other than what he had first designed.

Chapter Twenty-Six

Pentecostal Churches

Pentecostal churches believe that baptism is in the name of Jesus Christ. Their only goal is to spread the message of Jesus Christ, that He is the Lord of all people in the world. Pentecostal church doctrine and practice are as follows: they rejected the Trinitarian understanding of God; they stress the life of holiness, holding believers accountable for His sanctification and full participation in salvation. They maintained water baptism and the Lord's Supper with wine and bread.

Pentecostal's believed that only the King James Bible is accepted as the Word of God. They maintained that doctrine of salvation, divine healing, baptism in the Holy Spirit with the speaking in tongues, and the Second Coming of Jesus Christ are fully strongly emphasized. Mission work is also conducted in many countries. Pentecostal churches were established in 1901 from then on the Assembly of God continues. Scripture is inspired and without error according to their preaching and teaching as well as their doctrine. So church people of Pentecostal churches view certain leaders as prophets with authoritative messages that are to be confirmed from the Scriptures. Pentecostal's doctrine teaches that there is only one God, the Creator and one Lord of all, who exist eternally as the Trinity: Father, Son and Holy Spirit. The Son is eternal incarnate, fully human and fully God, conceived and born of the virgin Mary, died on the Cross for humanity's sins, rose bodily from the grave, to Heaven, and will return to judge people of this Earth. Pentecostal churches teach that we are saved by God's grace, by faith in Christ alone, resulting in our being born again to new life in the Spirit as evidence by a life of holiness.

Pentecostal teach that the souls of believers upon dying go straight immediately to be with the Lord; and at Christ's return their bodies are raised to immortal, eternal life. The wicked will suffer eternal punishment in punishment in Hell. Pentecostal churches teach baptism of immersion of believers only, as a symbol of their faith in Christ. The Lord's Supper is a symbolic memorial of Christ's death and anticipation of His return. Pentecostal church believe that the Church is the body of Jesus Christ, in which the Holy Spirit dwells, which meets to worship God, and which is the agency for bringing the Gospel of salvation to the entire people in the world. Pentecostal is very strict in the sense of speaking in tongues; they view it as the evidence of initial baptism in the Holy Spirit which they believe that it is the second work of grace to sanctification; some charismatic accept speaking in tongues, but they do not view it as the only initial evidence of the baptism in the Holy Spirit.

"Then the word of the Lord came to me. O house of Israel, can I not do with you as this potter does? Declares the Lord. Like clay in the hand of potter, so are you in my hand, O house of Israel. If at any time I announce that a nation or kingdom is to be uprooted, turn down and destroyed, and If that nation I warned repents of its evil, then I will relent and not inflict on it the disaster I had planned" (Jeremiah 18 : 5-7). This parable contains several important principles of God's work in the lives of his people. Our submission to God as the One who molds both our character and our service to Him determine to a large extent what He can do with us.

Grace D. Balogun

Chapter Twenty-Seven

What Can Make All Churches Be One?

There are two main major denominations in the world - The Protestants and the Catholic Churches. Whereby between those two we have a break down by several different branches of Catholic churches, and several different Protestant churches in the world. There are some churches who see all religions have been equal in Christ, and that all the people attending and worshiping in this church exercise no bias mind against other church. An example of this is the Unitarian Church.

The evangelicals that are most centered in Christ, state that Christ said, "I am the bread of life. He who comes to me will never go hungry, and he who believes in me will never be thirsty" (John 6:35). Jesus Christ is the bread of life, this is the first of His seven sayings of, "I am" statements recorded in the Gospel of John which or where each "I am" an important aspect of the personal ministry of Jesus Christ. The statement tells us that Christ is the sustenance that nourishes spiritual life. Our Lord also said: "I am the way and the truth and the life. No one comes to the Father except through me" (John 14:6).

We as a believing Christians must pray in Jesus' name, pray in harmony with His nature, with His character, and with His will. Christians must pray in Christ's name with faith in Him and in His authority as well as with a desire to glory both the Father and the Son. "By faith in the name of Jesus, this man whom you see and know was made strong. It is Jesus' name and faith that comes through him that has given this complete healing to him, as you can all see" (Acts 3:16). Apostle Peter was telling the people here that faith and prayer in Jesus' name can heal and do a miraculous thing in people's life as we are in Christ. There should be no discrimination against, or between one denomination to another denomination, if we all study, follow the teaching of Jesus Christ which He laid down before He ascended to Heaven.

In the early Church era prayer was the first and most important priority and an integral part of their life. Together, prayer was the tool that kept the bond of unity and the key to their bond of peace. If all the Christians pray more and more every day, they will not have time to find fault against each other, the focus is on the Lord Jesus the Head, the foundation of the Church. All the Churches of Christ will concentrate on how to make disciples for Christ. Praying in the name of Jesus Christ, therefore, means that Jesus will answer any prayer that He would have prayed Himself. There is no limitation to the power of prayer if all the denominational churches in the world pray and address to Jesus or the Father in holy faith according to His desire. Christ Jesus, during His earthly ministry, was preaching: "He replied, 'Because you have so little faith. I tell you the truth, if you have faith as small as a mustard seed, you can say to this mountain, move from here to there and it will move. Nothing will be impossible for you" (Matthew 17:20-21). Our Lord and Savior Jesus Christ always and frequently made comments on the nature of true faith. He speaks of a faith that can move mountains, faith that can make big miracles and healing, and that can accomplish great things for God.

The faith that we prayed for the believers is the true faith, which is effective faith that produces results that bring great changes to believer's life. True faith exercises force, with power, but faith in God. True faith, which manifests from the work of God within the hearts of all believing Christians, which involves awareness that is divinely imparted to believers hearts' so that our prayers are answered. The Holy Spirit will be able to create within the believers what they cannot produce in their worn minds.

"And if at another time I announce that a nation or kingdom is to be built up and planted, and if it does evil in my sight and does not obey me, then I will reconsider the good I had intended to do for it" (Jeremiah 18:9-10). God the Father Almighty remains free to change His pronounced decisions and to regulate His dealings with us according to our response to His offer of forgiveness or to His threat of judgment.

Grace D. Balogun

Chapter Twenty-Eight

Why Do We Have Different Doctrine?

Catholics teach that their members should pray to Mary, the mother of God, the Son, Jesus Christ. They believe that Mary is equal to Jesus and their members should pray to her as well pray to other saints. This is not the teaching of the Apostle Peter who was the Papal of the Catholic Church; this was not in the teaching or preaching of the early Church. Where do they get this from, because it is not in the Old Testament teaching of coming of the Messiah and it was not in the teaching Jesus Christ during His earthly ministry. Jesus Christ mentioned the Holy Spirit after His ascension. He did not mention any one else, not Mary, His mother, not any of His brothers or sisters. Catholic doctrinal priests know that God says: "And God spoke all these words: I am the Lord you God, who brought you out of Egypt, out of the land of slavery. You shall have no other gods before me" (Exodus 20:1-2). The Ten Commandments were written in God's own hands on two stones tablets and given to Moses and the children of Israel. Are we going to put the Ten Commandment aside and worship Mary as God? Keeping the commandments provides a way for Israel and all the believing Christians to respond righteously to God in the spirit of gratitude for delivering us from all our past, present and future sins. Christ and the apostles affirm that, as valid expressions of God's holy will, the commandment must remain an obligatory for all the New Testament believers.

Catholic Churches should not have included the worshiping of Mary. In this respect, they're not following God's commandments summed up by the love for God and love for one's neighbor; It is also empowered the believers to fulfill the righteous requirements of the law by loving God and others from our hearts. To love God, our Maker and Redeemer, with love that demands our inner spiritual righteousness that expressed in outward justice and holiness. Mary is the messenger, servant of God, to carry out the purposes of God on this Earth by bringing our Lord Jesus Christ into this world through the power of the Holy Spirit who empowered Mary to conceive, and be born by the virgin Mary. Who says, "From now on people will call me blessed." God prohibited the polytheism that characterized all the religions of ancient people near or far not to worship, or call on any of the gods of their nations, but was commanded to fear the Lord and serve Him only.

Believing Christians must direct their worship to God in Christ alone. They must not worship, pray, or seeking guidance and help from any other gods, any spirit, or worship of the dead as Catholic people worship the saints and those who are dead. God commanded all His children not to bow down for any other gods

,either the worship of demons through Spiritism, divination and other forms of idolatry; all the believers must be solely consecrated to God, who only through His will and through His inspired Word, faithfully guide their lives.

Lord Jesus Christ let the Catholic officials come to this Scripture's realization and stop worshiping Mary and worship "God the Father, God the Son, and God the Holy Spirit." Although, Mary told Jesus in the wedding at Canaan that the bridegroom ran out of wine, but you still help them according to your time, therefore, if the Catholic's wanted to use that as the reason to worship Mary, let them realize that you are our great intercessor on Earth. Mary cannot be our intercessor; when we can come straight to You boldly, approach the Throne of grace directly by ourselves and you as our great intercessor in Heaven, You have to intercede for us and pray for those who believe in You with prayer that can never be uttered.

"God is not a man, that he should change his mind. Does he speak and then not act? Does he promise and not fulfill? I have received a command to bless; he has blessed, and I cannot change it" (Numbers 23:19-20). Things are not predetermined and unalterable, not even in the mind of God. He takes into account spiritual changes in His people. God does not change within Himself; He retains the right to change His mind and alter His declared promises and threats. People of this Earth should never accept a theology that denies God this sovereign freedom.

Chapter Twenty-Nine

What Can We Do To Make All Churches One in Christ?

All churches can be one if they all take every word of God in the Scripture seriously without complaint. All churches can be one if they follow divine authority of the Scripture. All churches can be one of that take the teaching and preaching of Jesus Christ as the final Word of worship, of living, of prayer, of witnessing, and in discipleship day to day until Christ returns. All churches shall be one if they have a unilateral form of worship. Some churches believe that dancing is the best way to worship the Lord and expresses their adoration and gratitude; while other denominational churches believes that the best way to worshiping is just singing praises to the Lord Jesus Christ is the best way to worship, while other denominational churches feel that standing up, raising two hands to Heaven and praying all day is the best way to worship. Another denominational church feels that the best way to worship and he or she can get answers quickly to their prayers is to lie down prostrate on the floor all day and cry to God for their problem, that is why some churches that practice lying prostrate down to worship have no chairs in the church or their assembly place. While some denominational churches believe that they have to read the Bible, or open the Bible to anywhere and God is speaking to them through any area that their Scripture opens to when they open the Bible, therefore, they read all days, or weeks in other to find answers to their problems or their hearts' desires.

Many denominational churches listen to preachers, all week, all day Sunday; they believe in the Scripture that says: "Where two or three people are gather together I will answered their prayers." They don't really pray on their own but they join other believers wherever they are praying. In other denominations you see people sit down silently without saying a word all day - claiming that they are trying to reach God through their mind, as well as trying to hear the voice of the Lord. While in some denominations they listen to Organ's "ressart" or openly play different kinds of music all day and said this is how they clear their mind from the world's pollution all week from what they go through all week. Some denominations speak in tongues all day, and said that they were empowered with the Holy Spirit, but they are not interpreting what they were saying so that the others in the congregation can be able to understand them. Other denominational churches weep all day for their sins and feel that it is the best way to worship the Lord Jesus Christ. Other denominational Church stop at the crucifixion of the Lord Jesus

Christ and feel sad all day; they are not going beyond the crucifixion and burial of the Lord. They don't believe in the resurrection of Jesus Christ so that they can rejoice.

All the churches can be one if they decided to follow one form of worship without diverting to so many ways of worship. They will be one if they worship as the early believing Christians churches worship during the Apostle Era. The can be one in worship if they follow what the Scripture say about worshiping the Lord; with all our Mind, Spirit, soul and body. Churches can be one in Christ if they have one form of worshiping the Lord. but every one stop showing that their own way of worship is the best. Sometimes, people in the churches follow anything that pops up in their mind and they made the standard doctrine of that denomination. Anything that is not in the Scripture, in the Holy Bible from Old Testament to the New Testament; is a Man-Made Doctrine and it will not be approved of God.

In all the denominational churches and practices, they all believe that their doctrine is the best form that it will help people get close to the Lord. Some denominational churches do not believe in public worship, and will never attend any public worship, or prayers. Some families will not pray together because of the Scripture that says: "And when you pray, do not be like the Hypocrites, for they love to pray standing in the synagogues and on the street corners to be seen by men. I tell you the truth; they have received their reward in full. But when you pray, go into your room, closed the door and pray to your Father, who sees what is done in secret, will reward you" (Matthew 6:5-7). We are to realize that either we pray, worships in public or in our room it is between us and our Lord and Savior.

Incorporating public prayers cannot necessarily solve the problems of every notion or the problem of the world. All what the denominational churches need is the power of the Holy Spirit, the infusion of the Spirit in the churches in our home, city, states, in our country and in the entire world. With one form of contacting the Lord, approaching the Throne of grace all churches will be one in mouth and in deed.

"But the man of God answered the king, 'Even if you were to give me half your possessions, I would not go with you, nor would I eat bread of drink water here. For I was commanded by the word of the Lord: You must not eat bread or drink water or return by the way you came" (1st Kings 13:8-9). The word of the Lord came to the man of God, God's spokesman was under the highest obligation to follow the entire Word of the Lord. It is the same today with all the servants of the Lord. They must obey the commandment of the Lord.

Chapter Thirty

Who Is The Body of Christ?

All the converted believers are the body of Christ. Jesus Christ is the Head of the Church and we are part of His body, His flesh and His bones. The Lord Jesus Christ is to be glorified by our worship and adoration, which He receives from all the denominational churches. In the Book of Ephesians the Scripture revealed that: " There is one body and one Spirit just as you were called to one hope when you were called - one Lord, One Faith, one Baptism, One God and Father of all, who is over all and through all and in all" (Ephesians 4:4-6). We have to know that Jesus Christ is the Lord; there is no other. The unity of the Spirit cannot be created by any human being. It already exists for those who have believed the truth and have received Jesus Christ as the Apostle Paul proclaimed it in: (As a prisoner for the Lord, then, I urge you to live a life worthy of the calling you have received. Be completely humble and gentle; be patient, bearing with one another in love. Make every effort to keep the unity of the Spirit through the bond of peace" (Ephesians 4:1-3). Apostle Paul was telling the people of Ephesus, as believers, how to be one in Christ. Also, he is telling us today and until Jesus Christ returns to Earth. We must keep the unity, not through any human efforts, or through any organizations, it is by living a life worthy of our calling that Christ calls us and that we receive from Him. The Scriptural unity, which is maintained by our Loyalty to the truth and by keeping in step with the Spirit, it can never be attained, or achieved by any human efforts.

The Scripture revealed: "Are you so Foolish? After beginning with the Spirit, are you now trying to attain your goal by human efforts (Galatians 3:3)? All the believing Christians in this world receive the Holy Spirit, the empowerment of the Holy Spirit by faith in Jesus Christ, and all the blessings that follows. Anyone who seems to be justified by the Law does not receive the Spirit and he does not have Christ living in him or her because the Law cannot impart life into any human being. Therefore, we are the body of Christ, the One Lord, which is essential to all the believing Christians in faith and in unity. This is the confession that makes it clear that there is only one Lord means Jesus Christ's work of redemption is perfect and sufficient; there is no other redeemer, no other mediator for believers, we have a complete salvation through our Lord Jesus Christ. All the believing Christians are to draw near, close to Him as our Head, and through Jesus Christ our Savior to God. Jesus Christ alone is the way, the truth and the life, believing in Him we have eternal life, life everlasting.

"Who have been chosen according to the foreknowledge of God the Father, through the sanctifying work of the Spirit, for obedience to Jesus Christ and sprinkling by his blood" (1st Peter 1:2). We are the body of Christ, Jesus Christ is the Head of the Church. We have been chosen to be God's people according to His foreknowledge, according to God's own comprehensive knowledge of His plan of redemption in Christ for the Church, even before the foundation and creation of human history began.

Foreknowledge means God's sovereignty had far-seeing purpose for redeeming human kind according to His eternal love and plan. The chosen ones are all the believers of Jesus Christ in the world. The true believers chosen in harmony with God's determinable plan to redeem the Church by the blood of Jesus Christ through the Spirit's sanctifying word. All believers must be able to participate in their election by their response of faith and by being eager to make their calling and election sure. Believers are shielded by the power of God against Satan's sinister forces of evil that seek to destroy their lives and salvation in Christ. The body of Christ exercises faith, which is the essential requirement of God's protection. God's shielding all the body of Christ by His grace does not work arbitrarily, for only through faith believers are protected by God's power, just as only through faith the body of Christ are saved. Therefore, living faith in Christ as Lord and Savior is the present responsibility in maintaining and remaining in God's continued protection of the body of Christ. Christ is in the believer and believers are in Christ. The body of Christ is one in

Jesus Christ, nothing can pull them apart, and they have been sealed with the Holy Spirit empowerment. The goal of God's protection through the believers' faith is salvation through the atoning sacrifice of Jesus Christ. God the Father Almighty considers the faith of the body of Christ means today's believers as a greater wonder than the faith of those who saw and lead Jesus in person during His earthly ministry, even after His resurrection. Christ said: "Blessed are those who have not seen but their faith is constant." Believers now, although, they have never seen him, love him and believe in him." (John 20:29) Our Lord Jesus said: there is a special blessing for those who have not seen and yet have believed. As we live by faith we are given joy as God's gift to us.

The body of Christ has been sanctifying sanctification, which may involves a holy encounter with God after the initial salvation. Believers of Jesus Christ may receive a clear revelation of God's holiness as well as a consciousness that God is calling them to separate them in a greater way from sin and from the sinful world and for a holy, intimate relationship with the living God. All the believers, the body of Christ therefore, must present themselves to God as a living sacrifice and receive from the Holy Spirit grace, purity and enabling power to live holy lives that are pleasing to God - God the Father delights and rejoices when He transforms sinners in to a child of God - into the body of Christ.

Acknowledging who Christ is in our lives will help us to know that Christ is our Head; we are part of His body, His flesh and His bone on Earth. We are Christ's body. There is only one body according to the Scripture: "Far above all rule and authority, power and dominion, and every title that can be given, not only in the present age but also in the one to come. And God placed all things under his feet and appointed him to be head over everything for the Church" (Ephesians 1:21-22). God put everything under the rule of Jesus Christ. He is the Head of the Church. We are the body of Jesus Christ, and we are the only churches that belong to Christ. And in Colossians the Scripture revealed: "And he is the head of the body, the Church, he is the beginning and the first born from among the dead, so that in everything he might have the supremacy. For God was pleased to have all his fullness dwell in him, and through him to reconcile to himself all things whether things on earth or things in heaven; by making peace through his blood, shed on the cross" (Colossians 1:18-20).

    God Almighty created all things both materials and spiritual in Heaven and on Earth owed their existence to Jesus Christ's redemptive work in all creation to Jesus as the active agent in this universe. Jesus Christ was the first to rise from the dead, no one before Him, no one after with a spiritual and immortal body. On the day of resurrection Jesus Christ became the Head of the Church. Then New Testament Church began on the day of resurrection when the disciples received the Holy Spirit. Jesus Christ is the firstborn from among the dead; He is the resurrection of all those whom He died to save and rose from the dead. The body of Christ is those who Jesus came to this Earth to save and redeem from their sins and sin nature. The body of Christ are those who believe in Him and gave their life to him live for Him forever physically and spiritually belongs to Jesus Christ, as well as committing to follow His teaching, abide in Him, and who makes themselves one in Him, as He is one with the Father.

"Dear Friend, I pray that you may enjoy good health and that all may go well with you, even as your soul is getting along well" (3rd John 1:2). It is God's provision and intention that we as believers of Jesus Christ must be in good health and that our lives be accompanied by His blessings. He wants all to go well with us our work, plans, purposes in life, ministry, and our families. God wants our entire lives to go well according to God's will and direction for us.

Chapter Thirty - One

Speaking In Tongues

The book of 1st Corinthians, chapter twelve teaches all the believers about all the spiritual gifts of believers. Apostle Paul said: "I do not want you to be ignorant. There are different kinds of gifts, but the same Spirit. There are different kinds of service, but the same Lord. There are different kinds of working but the same God works all of them in all men. To each one the manifestation of the Spirit is given for the common good. The one there is give through the Spirit the message of wisdom, to another the message of knowledge by means of the same Spirit, to another faith by the same Spirit, to another gifts of the healing by that one Spirit, to another miraculous powers, to another prophecy, to another distinguishing between spirits, to another speaking in different kinds of tongues, and to still another the interpretation of tongues. All these are the work of one and the same Spirit, and he gives them to each one, just as he determines" (1st Corinthians

12:1, 4-11). The gifts of the Holy Spirit, or the manifestation of the Holy Spirit in the life of the body of Christ Jesus for the mutual good of all the body of Christ. The gifts of the Holy Spirit and the manifestation of the Spirit were an indispensable part of the early Church's life and ministry.

God the Father intended that these spiritual gifts continue in operation until the return of Christ to Earth. The purposes of the Spiritual gifts of the believers are as follows: (1) to manifest the grace of God, the power and the love of the Spirit among the believers in their public gatherings, either at home with the family and in individual lives. The gifts of the Holy Spirit is to help the teachers and the preachers of the Word of God such as pastors, ministers, who witness Spirit empower them to make the preaching and teaching of the Gospel effective by giving them supernatural confirmation to the message of God. Spiritual gifts is to meet all the human needs and to strengthen and build them up for the Church spiritually and to make individual believers perfect in love that comes from a pure heart and a good conscience with sincere faith. The gift of spiritual gifts will help individual or corporate church to wage spiritual war against Satan and all the forces of evil in the world.

Spiritual gifts specify their nature, and it refers to supernatural manifestation that comes as gifts from the Holy Spirit operating through believers for the common good. To be clear and precise, according to the Scripture, spiritual gifts involve both in inward activities, actualized, and enablement, which is received from the Spirit of God; such as gift of spiritual strength of the body of Christ and those in need of spiritual help. The ministry service emphasizes that there are different ways of service and that certain gifts involve receiving the ability and power to help others. This same ministry aspect of the gifts reflects the servanthood ministry of our Lord Jesus Christ. Therefore, the operation of the gifts is defined in terms of Christ's presence and operation among the believers. The working or the effect of the gifts of the Holy Spirit signifies that spiritual gifts are in direct operation of the power of God the Father Almighty, which produces numerous results. The manifestations of the Holy Spirit emphasizes that spiritual gifts are direct manifestations of the work activities of and the presence of the Holy Spirit in the believers.

Speaking in different kinds of tongues means speaking in many different languages. It is a supernatural manifestation of the Spirit. Tongues may be in form of an existing language or an unknown language in the world. Speech that no one has known, or has been learned it is always difficult for the speaker and to the hearer because they don't know what the speaker is saying and no one can interpret it. Speaking in tongues always involves the human spirit and the Spirit of God which join together so that believer communicates directly to God for prayer, praises, blessings or thanksgiving. It is an expression or utterance at the level of one's spirit rather than the mind and praying for themselves and others under the direction, influence of the Holy Spirit apart from the activity of the mind. Tongues speaking in the congregational Church must be accompanied by a Spirit given interpretation that communicates the content and meaning of the utterance to the Christian believers. Tongues sometimes contain a revelation, knowledge, prophecy, or teaching for the assembly for the people in the congregational church just as Apostle Paul stated in the Scripture: "If anyone speaks in a tongue, two or at the most three should speak, one at a time, and someone must interpret. If there is no interpreter, the speakers should keep quiet in the church and speak to himself and God" (1st Corinthians 14:27-28). In the congregational church speaking in tongues must be regulated, otherwise the speaker may be out of control. In the use of spiritual gifts there must be an order and regulations.

The Scriptural guide for speaking in tongues within the denominational church is that if any, in any assembly, there must be an interpreter whether praising the Lord or praying, it must be done by one person at a time. All speaking in tongues must be judged by the church as to the authenticity. If there is no interpreter, the speaker must be speaking in tongues privately in prayer to God. Speaking in tongues is a spiritual gift; it's a spirit given ability to understand and communicate the language when interpreted for the congregation.

Tongues function either as a directive worship, prayer, or prophecy. The body of all the believing Christians can participate in the Spirit inspired revelation. Interpretation of tongues can be a gift, or means of edification as the entire congregation responds to the utterance. The gift may be given to the person who speaks in tongues or to someone else. There are some denominational churches that don't believe in tongues. Some other denominational churches stated that it was for the apostle's only, not for the believers of today. They believe that God gave the apostles the ability so that they could witness to people who were in Jerusalem on the Day of Pentecost may understand them, in their individual language. Therefore, speaking in tongues is not approved in other congregational denominations.

"It gave me great joy to have some brothers come and tell about your faithfulness to the truth and how you continue to walk in the truth" *(3rd John 1:3)* All the believing Christians should trust God to supply all our needs materially, we must recognized the Bible's teaching that we may sometimes experience need in order to be encouraged to trust him more and to develop our faith, spiritual endurance in our ministry.

Chapter Thirty - Two

Miracle of the Healing Power of Christ

Many denominational churches do not believe in the power of miracle healings today. They claim that it is for the apostle era. They forget that our Lord and Savior Jesus Christ said that: many denominational churches don't not believe in the miracle power of healing today. Miracle means something that happens amazingly and wonderfully unexpected. It is a manifestation of the supernatural work of God in the lives of believers. Jesus Christ's miracles are very significant and it was done in order to prove that He was indeed the Son of the Most High God. His miracles also prove that Jesus Christ has complete control over all what He created in Heaven and on Earth. Christ's disciples were the witness of all what Christ did on Earth, especially His miracle of healing. Jesus Christ did miracles of healing such as curing diseases or illnesses, casting out demons and evil spirits from those people who possess them. Christ's miracle power of healing was for those that were disabled, distressed, suffering with illness or disease during His earthly ministry on Earth. The dead were raised to life again by His word. Therefore, Jesus Christ's miracle power of healing gave validity to His ministry. Christ was a Great Physician, the Healer of those who believed in Him during His earthly ministry. Jewish Pharisees and Sadducees, including the ruler of the synagogues – the Sanhedrin, knew about Jesus' power of healing, but they failed to acknowledge it or they were jealous about it because of their position. Jesus Christ healed all those who were brought to Him with no exception. Christ's ability to heal everyone no matter who they are made Him a unique and great healer that the world has ever known.

  The Scripture revealed: " A man with leprosy came to him and begged him on his knees, if you are willing, you can make me clean. Filled with compassion, Jesus reached out his hand and touched the man, I am willing, he said. 'Be clean,' immediately the leprosy left him and he was cured" (Mark 1:40-45). Jesus' healing power was used to prove His claim to the world that He is the promised Messiah. The Scripture also revealed the faith of those Jesus healed. Their faith took part in Christ's healing miracles. "When Jesus had entered Capernaum, a centurion came to him, asking for help. Lord, he said, my servant lies at home paralyzed and in terrible suffering. Jesus said to him, 'I will go and heal him.' The centurion replied, 'Lord just say the word, and my servant will be healed.' When Jesus heard this, he was astonished and said to those following him, 'I tell you the truth, and I have not found anyone in Israel with such great faith. I say to you that many will come from the East and from the West, and will take their places at the feast with Abraham, Isaac and Jacob in the kingdom of heaven. But the subjects of the kingdom will be thrown outside, into the darkness, where there will be weeping and gnashing of teeth" (Matthew 8:5-7, 10-12). We see here that faith surpassed anything that Christ Jesus found among the Israelites. Faith combined with a loving concern for another person with great trust in Christ. The healing of the centurion servant warns all the believers that we may be excluded from what God is doing by adhering to human traditions of by failing to believe in the power of Christ's Kingdom.

The dead were restored to life by Jesus. "Soon afterward, Jesus went to a town called Nain, and his disciples and a large crowd went along with him. As he approached the town gate, a dead person was being carried out, the only son of his mother, and she was a widow. And a large crowd from the town was with her. When the Lord saw her, his heart went out to her and he said, 'Don't cry.' Then he went up and touched the coffin, and those carrying it stood still. He said, 'Young man, I say to you, get up!' The dead man sat up and began to talk, and Jesus gave him back to his mother" (Luke 7:11-15). Believing Christians could see clearly our Lord's compassion for the widow and her son; it shows that God has a special love and care for the widows, or for any person who is left alone in the world. God is a Father to those who were fatherless and he also a defender, provider for the widows. God put them under His special care and protection by means of the tithe offering and the abundance of His people. Our Lord blesses those who help and honor them. God Almighty is against those who take advantage of the widows or those who hurt them, to include the orphans. Widows are the apple eye of God's tender love mercies and compassion. The early Church made it a number one priority to care for widows. One important aspect of faith is to look after the orphans and widows in their distresses and troubles and care for them. Our Lord said: All the denominational churches must believe in the miracle power of Jesus healing because it is part of Jesus' work during His earthly ministry. The Scripture revealed: "He replied. 'Because you have so little faith. I tell you the truth, if you have faith, as small as a mustard seed, you can say to this mountain, move from here to there and it will move. Nothing will be impossible for you" (Matthew 17:20-21).

Faith is very important in following Christ; believers must have faith in Him. Jesus Christ comments constantly on the nature of true faith. He speaks of faith that can move mountains. Faith that can cause the miracles and healing and accomplish great things for the Lord. The faith that Jesus is referring to is the true faith; it is an effective faith that produces good results. This faith can force the power of God to be manifest in the lives of believers. Our Lord said in the Scripture, "I tell you the truth, anyone who has faith in me will do what I have been doing. He will do even greater things than those, because I am going to the Father. And I will do whatever you ask in my name, so that the Son may bring glory to the Father. You may ask me for anything in my name, and I will do it" (John 14: 12-14).

    Our Lord Jesus gave us His word that those who believe in Him will do the same work He did and they will do a greater work. Jesus Christ's desire is to see all believers to do the works that He did. The greater thing that our Lord mentioned is to convert the people, non-believers to Christ. We are to be the holy hands of Christ and perform miracles of healing that can make a nonbeliever to know that definitely Christ in you is the hope of glory. The reason for believers to do greater things done by the disciples is that Christ will go to His Father, and send forth power of the Holy Spirit as well as answer prayer in His name. Greater work will also include evangelizing the people of the whole world. Believers must pray in Jesus' name in order to achieve greater things for Him in His name. All denominational churches must believe and practice, as well as pray for the power of miracles of healing the sick, disabled, the distressed, also, wake up the dead.

"I have no greater joy than to hear that my children are walking in the truth" (3rd John 1:4.) God's presence, help and blessings in our physical lives are related to the prosperity of our spiritual lives. All Believing Christians must seek God's will to obey the Holy Spirit, remain separated from the spirit of this evil world; and love God's Word.

Chapter Thirty - Three

What Is Christ's Commandment To The Church?

One of the important and necessary commandments and instruction of our Lord is that believers must pray in Jesus' name. We still have many denominational churches that do not pray in Jesus' name. They will mention God, but they will not specify which God. Many denominational churches will say that they believe in God, but they don't believe in Jesus; that Jesus is their brother, not God. Some will say; they believe in Jesus, but they don't believe in Jesus Christ and they can be calling Jesus a hundred times without mentioning His full name. In order for all the churches to be one in Christ, they must pray in Jesus Christ's name. Prayer in Jesus' name involves two important things. All the churches must pray in harmony with Christ's nature, character and pray according to His will. All the denominational churches must pray in faith in Christ and in His authority and with the desire to glorify the Father and the Son with the power of the Spirit of

God's indwelling. Praying in the name of Jesus, therefore, means that Jesus will answer any prayer that He would have prayed by Himself. There is no limit to the power of prayer when we offered it directly to Jesus Christ or to God the Father in holy faith according to His desire.

Jesus Christ instructs all the Christian believers that the Holy Spirit is the Spirit of Truth. "If you love me, you will obey what I command. And I will ask the Father, and he will give you another Counselor to be with you forever - The Spirit of truth. The world cannot accept him, because it neither sees him nor knows him. But you know him, for he lives with you and will be in you. I will not leave you as orphans. I will come to you before long, the world will not see me anymore, but you will see me. Because I live, you will live" (John 14:15-19). Jesus instructs the disciples that He will ask the Father to give all believers the Counselor, only to those who are serious about their love for Him and their devotion to His Word. Jesus Christ commanded the believers and emphasized the importance of His presence in the life of believing Christians and a continuing attitude of love and obedience to His teaching and commandment. The Holy Spirit, the comforter, will be with all the believing Christians to help them and strengthen them, to teach and preach the true course for their lives as well as to comfort them in time of difficult situations; to intercede in prayer for them and to be a good intimate friend better than an earthly friend. The Holy Spirit will help the believers to further their best interest and will remain with them forever. Jesus Christ's instruction made this clear with His love. Christ said that the Holy Spirit that lives with the disciples will also live with all those who believe in Him and gave their life to Him. Christ promises them that in the future He will be in them. This is the promise of the indwelling of the Holy Spirit, which was fulfilled on the Day of Pentecost. All the denominational churches must follow the instruction of Christ and the command of Christ in order to be one in Him and for all churches to be one.

Christ breathed on the disciples after His resurrection and said to them, 'Receive the Holy Spirit." Again Jesus said, 'Peace be with you as the Father has sent me, I am sending you.' " And with that he breathed on them and said, 'Receive the Holy Spirit. If you forgive anyone his sins, they are forgiven; if you do not forgive them, they are not forgiven" (John 20: 21-22). Jesus Christ our Lord and Savior will reveal Himself to the obedient believer through the Holy Spirit, who makes known the personal presence of Jesus Christ God the Father the only one who is full of love to all His people. All the churches will be one if all churches follow the commandment of the Savior and His Word. They will all, with one accord, glorify the Father of light, Son and the Holy Spirit. They will also adopt one unifying form of worship with true holiness hearts.

"Dear friends, let us love one another, for love comes from God. Everyone who loves has been born of God and knows God. Whoever does not love does not know God, because God is love" *(1st John 4:7-8)* All Christian believers must love one another. Love is one important aspect of the fruit of the Spirit and it is an evidence of the re-birth.

Chapter Thirty - Four

Why Do Churches Condemn Each Other?

Churches condemn each other because every denominational church feel that they are the best. They turn the Church of Jesus Christ into a competitive store - everyone claiming that they know everything. Everyone, instead of following the Word of Christ, the teaching of Christ, the commandment of Jesus Christ; they derive their own doctrine. They turn the Holy Bible upside down and pick what they feel that their congregation wants to hear. They are making congregations in thousands, but they are not making disciples and they are not converting souls into the Kingdom of God. Some church's officials scream if they see anyone enter their church with the holy cross chain on their neck, or anywhere on their dress; they will start screaming and yelling, "He is no longer on the cross, take that cross off from your neck, or from your dress." Some of them will even be saying, "Take it out of here and throw it in the garbage." If you are trying to explain to them, that this is the basis why we were saved, and they must remember that if Christ did not go to the Cross, no one would have been saved, they will tell you to forget about the Cross. This is a wrong teaching; these ministers and pastors are not following the Scriptures because nowhere in the Scripture does it say to forget about the Cross. This means they are telling the believer to forget about the work of redemption of God the Father through God the Son. Some denominational churches will never put the Cross in their assembly, and there are no signs of the Cross of Christ anywhere. If you ask them, they will say that they don't believe in the Cross.

While on the other hand, other denominational churches will not observe the Lord's Supper: "For I received from the Lord what I also passed on to you: The Lord Jesus, on the night he was betrayed, took bread, and when he had given thanks, he broke it and said, 'This is my body, which is for you; do this in remembrance of me.' In the same way, after supper he took the cup saying, 'This cup is the new covenant in my blood do this, whenever you drink it, in remembrance of me. For whenever you eat this bread and drink this cup, you proclaim the Lord's death until he comes' " (1st Corinthians 11:23-26).

The Lord's Supper is very significant as it relates to the past, to the present and to the future of believers in the life of Jesus Christ. To the past significance because it is a remembrance of Christ's death for the humanity's redemptive work of sin and condemnation. Through the Lord's Supper we are once again confronted with the saving death of Christ and His redemptive significance for believers' lives. Christ's death is our ultimate motivation against falling into sin and for abstaining from all form of appearance of evil. It is a Thanksgiving for the blessings and salvation of God made available by Jesus Christ's sacrifice on the Cross. The present significance is that the Lord's Supper is a fellowship with Christ and a participation in the benefits of His sacrificial death, as well as a fellowship with the other believers of the body of Christ. In this Supper with the risen Lord, He as the host, becomes present in a special way. It is a recognition and proclamation of the New Covenant by which believers reaffirm the Lordship of Christ and our commitment to do His will, to remain loyal, to resist sin and to identify ourselves with His mission. The future significance of the Lord Supper's is a foretaste of the future Kingdom of God and the future Messianic banquet when all believers will be with the Lord. The future significance looks forward to Christ's imminent return for His people that dramatize prayers of "Your Kingdom come."

All the Lord's Supper's significance are meaningful, only if all the denominational churches come before the Lord in true faith, sincere prayer and with commitment to God's Word and to His will. Some churches refuse to observe the Lord's Supper; it was taken out of their way of worship and service. But they will engage in feet washing. Many denominational churches do not believe in fasting and prayer, claiming that fasting was ordered in the Old Testament and to the early churches in the New Testament, but not for today's believers. The worst thing is that some denominational churches condemned women preaching or teaching. They hold on to Apostle Paul's correction of what happened at the Corinthian Church, the fighting and confusions between women and the other men in the church that made Paul to tell the women to be silent in the church. "For I received from the Lord what I also passed on to you."

The Holy Bible Scriptures speaks specifically about Christ's agony on the Cross. "When the soldiers crucified Jesus, they took his clothes, dividing them into four shares, one for each of them, with the undergarment remaining. This garment was seamless, woven in one piece from top to bottom. Later, knowing that all was now completed, and so that the Scripture would be fulfilled, Jesus said, 'I am thirsty,' when he had received the drink, Jesus said, 'It is finished.' with that, he bowed his head and gave up his spirit" (John 19: 28-30). Jesus said, "It is finished," the work of redemption is complete. It is finished is a sound of triumph declaring the completed and accomplished work of the Cross. It is finished is a word of proclamation that the accomplished fact of Jesus Christ's earthly mission given to Him by His Father was all accomplished, the fulfillment of both Old Testament and the New Testament prophecy about the suffering Messiah. In the completed work of redemption; Christ the sacrificial and Passover Lamb of God who takes away the sin of the world with His own atoning blood on the Cross. Still some denominational churches do not want to hear anything about the

Cross and they do not want to display any sign of Cross in their assembly place.

These denominational churches that are the enemy of the Cross of Christ must go and read the Scripture again so that they can know that our salvation was completed on the Cross. Washing the feet: "So he got up from the meal, took off his outer clothing, and wrapped a towel around his waist. After that, he poured water into a basin and began to wash his disciple's feet, drying them with the towel that was wrapped around him. Now that I, your Lord and teacher, have washed your feet, you also should wash one another's feet. I have set you an example that you should do as I have done for you. I tell you the truth, no servant is greater than his master, nor is a messenger greater than the one who sent him. Now that you know these things, you will be blessed if you do them" (John 13:4-5, 14-17). The early Church followed Jesus' example and literally obeyed His admonition to humbly wash one another's feet in love. For example: "and is well known for her good deeds, such as bringing up children, showing hospitality, washing the feet of the saints, helping those in trouble and devoting herself to all kinds of good deeds" (1st Timothy 5:10). During the early Church in the New Testament, the widows were required to demonstrate certain spiritual qualifications including perseverance in good works. The dramatic action of washing the feet occurred on the last night of our Lord's life on Earth.

Christ demonstrated to His disciples how much He loved them; to foreshadow His self-sacrifice on the Cross; and to convey the truth that He was calling His disciples to serve one another in the spirit of humility. The Passion to be great had continually troubled the disciples. Jesus Christ wants them to see that the desire to be first, to be superior and honored above fellow Christians is contrary to the spirit of their Lord. Our Lord was demonstrating how Christians should take each other as one in Him - one body of Christ.

Grace D. Balogun

"This is how God showed his love among us: he sent his one and only Son into the world that we might live through him. This is love; not that we loved God, but that he loved us and sent his Son as an atoning sacrifice for our sins" (1st John 4:9-10). According to the Scripture, love is something that we are responsible to develop in our life. For this reason John exhorts us to love each other, to be concerned about them and to seek their welfare. We should love our neighbors, Apostle John urges us to demonstrate the love of God as children of God.

Chapter Thirty - Five

Churches Misinterpretation of the Work of Christ

There are many denominational churches that complained about what the other denominational churches are doing. They also hate them, especially where women are pastors. They condemn these churches, claiming that God did not call women to preach, and that women must not preach to men. They forget that women were the first teachers; they trained and raised their children according to the admonition of the will of God. Men will not, or almost never are around to train, raise their children, take the children to church, and then look for the welfare of their children, so that their children will know the Lord from the beginning of their life to the end.

Some churches believe, and it is in their doctrine, that women cannot teach the Scripture and that they cannot be a pastor. "For false Christ's and false prophets will appear and perform great signs and miracles to deceive even the elect - if that were possible. See, I have told you ahead of time"(Matthew 24:24-25).

Grace D. Balogun

Our Lord and Savior was warning all believing Christians as well as urging them continually to test the Spirit, energizing all teachers, leaders and preachers about the deception that is going to test the love of believers for Him and loyally to the truth of the Scriptures. The period of the deception will not be easy; it is going to cause a lot of confusion. Many denominations will be preaching for the sake of money. They will not allow women to serve the Lord as they should; they will condemn and discriminate against women's ministry service of the Lord. They will go to all extents to oppress women in the service of the Lord. They will also discriminate against people wearing crosses on their neck. They will treat them as if they were performing abominations against Jesus Christ by wearing a cross. During the Last Day religious deceitfulness will be widespread in all the nation of Earth that will make it difficult even for the elect who will like to pray for the Holy Spirit, Spirit discernment, in order to discern between the truth and error. Many denominational churches that do not love, or care to know the truth, will be deceived.

They will have no opportunity to believe the truth of the Gospel: "The one who received the seed that fell among the thorns is the man who hears the Word, but the worries of this life and the deceitfulness of wealth choke it, making it unfruitful" (Matthew 13:22). All the denominational churches must study the Scripture and abide in the Word, keep steadfast to the commandment of Jesus Christ, saving souls to His Holy hands instead of discriminating, condemning against each other's doctrine and beliefs. Our Lord Jesus Christ teaches that there will be good and evil in His visible Kingdom throughout the entire world, especially among those who profess His name. There will be a compromise and worldliness that will lead to apostasy, as well as faithfulness and godliness that will lead to eternal life. At the end of this world, the wicked will be destroyed. Then the righteous will shine like the Sun in the Kingdom of their Father. At the end of the age Christians will condemn Christians; they will be proclaiming themselves instead of proclaiming the Gospel. Pastors will be exulting themselves instead of exulting our Lord and Savior, giving glory to themselves instead of giving glory to God through Jesus Christ's atoning sacrifice. Faithful believing Christians must always be alert to the subversive elements and individuals that Satan is planting within all parts of God's work. They will, in many ways act, look like true children of God, but are fake and false teachers, preachers of the gospel of God.

    The false teachers were once believers in Christ who had crossed over from death to life, but had sometime after word serviced their union with Christ and gone out of life back unto death. The Scripture reveals that the apostles of our Lord Jesus Christ foretold. They said to give; in the last times there will be scoffers who will follow their own ungodly desires. These are men who divide you, who follow mere natural instincts and do not have the Spirit. But you, dear friends, build yourselves up in your most holy faith and pray in the Holy Spirit (Jude 17-20). The Scripture said that all the believing Christians must defend and propagate the faith and resist false teaching in four ways. By building ourselves up in our most holy faith. The holy faith is the New Testament revelation handed down by Jesus Christ and the apostles. It requires the study of the Word of God and with a determined effort to know the truth and the teachings of the Scripture. Believing Christians should learn how to pray in the Spirit.

Praying in the Spirit will enable the power of the Holy Spirit, looking at the Spirit to inspire us, guide us, energize, sustain and help us to do our battle in our prayers, pray with one mind and praying with one Spirit. "Have you not discriminated among yourselves and become judges with evil thoughts?" (James 2:4) The poor are very special and precious to our Lord and Savior and to God the Father. Sometimes, it is the poor in this world who are the richest in faith, and in spiritual gifts and who in their need; cry out most of their lives intensely to Christ in sincere hunger for His presence, His mercy and crying out for His help.

True Christian believers who are economically depressed in this world learn that they cannot put their trust in the material things of this world, and material possessions. Therefore, they respond more and more to Jesus Christ's invitation that says: love me, "Come to me, all who are wary and burdened, and I will give you rest. Take my yoke upon you and learn from me, for I am gentle and humble in heart, and you will find rest for your souls, for my yoke is easy and my burden is Light"(Matthew 11:28-30). Jesus Christ calls all those who believe in Him to a gracious invitation and holy calling, come to all who are weary and burdened with the troubles of life and the sins of their own human nature. By coming to Jesus Christ, and becoming His disciples, His followers, His servants, following His teaching and His commandment, obeying His directions. Christ will make us free from our insurmountable burdens and He will give us believers, rest, peace and His Holy Spirit to lead us throughout our life. With this truth in our heart all Christian believers should be one in Him and follow His direction, which is in His Word.

Some denominations discriminate against Seven Day Adventist believers. These are the believers that worship on Saturday; they follow the weekly Sabbath Worship from the Old Testament meaning rest, ceasing from all your work on the seventh day of the week according to the Law of Moses, set apart as a day of ceasing from normal work and forgiving of oneself to rest and to worship of the Lord. Many denominational churches change the Sabbath of resting and ceasing to the resurrection Sunday.

There are strong reasons to believe that the principles of the resurrection Sunday, and Saturday Sabbath, have a validity permanently for Christians and that we should all still set aside one day in seven days as a day of rest and a day of worship our Lord God Almighty Father, Son and Holy Spirit who is the same God from the Old Testament to the New Testament.

The concept of a sacred day of rest was commanded before the Jewish Law. "God blessed the seventh day and made it Holy" (Genesis 2:3, Exodus 20:11). This indicated that from the time of creation, God wanted one day in seven day to be a source of blessings for every child of God, not only the Jewish people, but for every people in the world. Christ, during His earthly ministry told the ruler of the synagogues that the day of rest was given for our spiritual and for our physical well-being. "Then he said to them, 'The Sabbath was made for man, not man for the Sabbath. So the Son of man is Lord even of the Sabbath' " (Mark 2:27-28). The Scripture reveals that the Sabbath was instituted by God as a blessing for human beings. On the day of Sabbath all human beings are to refrain from their daily work worship and fellowship and seek the face of the Lord, His full presence, in an intimate relationship in order to keep ourselves physically and spiritually healthy in the Spirit of holiness so that we can be spiritually strong in Him and refresh our soul. Those who do not take one day of the week to worship God are self-righteous people in the world.

All Churches Be One

"Dear Friends, since God so loved us, we also ought to love one another. No one has ever seen God; but if we love one another, God lives in us and his love is made complete in us" (1st John 4:11-12) All Christian believers have a love nature of God, which He showed by giving His own Son for us. We have His nature because we are born of Him.

Grace D. Balogun

Chapter Thirty-Six

Religion

Religion is a powerful source of humanity's spiritual energy on Earth. Religion plays a major role in some of the violent hatred that is going on in the world. There is no unity of worship; there are many religious beliefs, siblings, fathers, and mothers kill their own children because differences of their religious beliefs. All in the name of God. God is one, the Creator, the Holy Trinity, the forever one God who dwell in an unapproachable light that darkness cannot comprehend. No one has ever seen God before, no one has ever died and come back to tell us that He has seen God face to face. God is the Almighty, is a Spirit; those who worship Him must worship Him in Spirit and in truth. Jesus Christ, the only begotten Son of God has declared Him, and He said we must worship God with a Spirit of holiness. How can humanity possess the Spirit of holiness if they are killing each other because of their religious beliefs. In every church or mosque, synagogue, temple of Hindu god, Sikhism, etc., people of this world should remember that all the religious organizations are human beings made of flesh and blood who decided to seek God and conclude that his own finding of God is in this way, just like Mohammed in the Islamic Religion; but all of them form all these religions in order to create peace in the world. People turn their motives, and their intensions into violence and confusion. The true religious is Christianity where God the Father sent His only begotten Son into the world to redeem humanity from their sins so that we will be able to worship God in the Spirit and in truth. Christ is the only ascended God.

All other founders of religious beliefs are in the graves of the Earth where they are buried. In other words, the religion we have the celebration when a new body being born, wedding, burial ceremony, prayer voluntarily gathered together to sing, pray, work, teach and learn about God of that religion. There is always the teaching of children on how to honor God, how to believe in God and pray to God. While adults learn how to live well, do good to themselves and to others, how to grow in wisdom, knowledge and understanding of life. Also how to be compassionate, help the poor, feed the hungry, clothe the naked, comfort those who sick and lonely, especially the Senior Citizens.

The Imams, Rabbis, Pastors, Priests and all other religious leaders teach and preach about peace in the world. With all these similarities of worship, there are many religions who are all out to kill for example: The terrorists, Al-Qaida, the Taliban and all other Islamic Terrorists, the Hindu worshipers kill other people of other religions just like the Islamic terrorists. My question is when does this act of violence stop? And when we will see each other as friends calling on the same God in a different ways? When are we going to know that God is one and God is love; He will never tell anyone to kill innocent people, enter their home while they were sleeping, kill everybody, kill all the children, kill their own child because he worships other Gods. God would not tell anyone to kill the people that He created in order for them to get to Heaven, just as we human beings will not allow anyone to destroy what we have in order for them to come and live with us. God is a great. God will never destroy what He created.

All Churches Be One

"We know that we live in him and he in us, because he has given us of his Spirit. And have seen and testify that the Father has sent his Son to be the Savior of the World" (1st John 4: 12-14). We know that God loves us and because of God's love for us, we have experienced His love, forgiveness and help. We are obligated to help others, even if it is at great cost to us.

Chapter Thirty - Seven

Other Denominational Churches' Doctrinal Ministry

Church of Jesus Christ of Latter Day Saints: Is the official name of the religion commonly called the Mormon Church. They believe that the Word of God, like the Bible – it is the Holy Scripture, similar to that of the Bible. According to their doctrine – after Christ's death, the Book of Mormon contains the history of God's plan, and God's dealing with the people living in Americas in 600 BC and 400 AD. The prophets in the Book of Mormon by name, Joseph Smith, obtained these ancient records in 1827 with the power of God he was able to translate the ancient writings into today's language; which says Jesus Christ is the divine redeemer and that living according to His gospel they can find peace and eternal happiness in this life and in the life to come.

They believe that Joseph Smith at age of 21 years old, an Angel named Moroni gave him the ancient records, which was written on the metal sheets of gold. God gave him the gift and the power to translate them, and the translation was done within three months – in 1830. God made Joseph Smith that a prophet, seer, revelator and translator in order to restore the Church of Jesus Christ in today's truth. Joseph Smith answered the call of the Lord; he was blessed to bring the Book of Mormon to the people of the world. The Book of Mormon focuses on Jesus Christ atoning sacrifice and the Gospel of God and eternal happiness. Jesus Christ is their Savior, faith in Christ; the Book of Mormon's purpose is to let the people of the world know that Jesus Christ is the eternal God, manifesting Himself unto all nations. The Book of Mormon recorded that many prophets saw Christ face to face personally including Apostle Paul; Jesus appeared to all Nephites after His resurrection, blessed them and taught them the Gospel. The Book of Mormon is not a replacement for the Bible; both books contain the gospel of God. The Book of Mormon talks about the Bible and confirmed the truth in the Bible.

In the Book of Mormon, people learn about the Gospel and covenant to serve others and about eternal salvation. They believe that they know God better, draw closer to Him, as well as know how to help others. They believe that the Book of Mormon, through prayer and humbleness, find out that the book is the Word of God, same as the Bible.

The Doctrine of Church of Jesus Christ of Latter-day Saints believe first and foremost that Jesus Christ is the Savior of the world and the Son of God. They have a diverse background and experiences; they are united by commitment to Jesus Christ. They share their testimony about their faith, and what faith in Jesus Christ means to them as individual members. Mormons are followers of Jesus Christ; they live to serve Him and teach and preach to others about Christ eternal life, which was from the Father through His son Jesus Christ, to all who believe and gave their life to Christ. They believe that Jesus Christ is the only way by which humanity could be able to return to live with God the Father in Heaven. The believe also that Jesus suffered, was crucified for sins of the people in the world, repentance and forgiveness mercy and grace for all those who gave their life to Him; Christ saves from sin and death. They believe that Jesus Christ will return to reign for a thousand years. They believe that Christ is the resurrection and the life. Baptism is a promise of a covenant that will make them to follow Christ and develop faith. They believe in the gift of the Holy Spirit, which is also known as a confirmation ceremony. Mormon Church doctrine teaches that the member must make good intimate relationship with the Lord. They used the Book of Mormon as their Bible and their second Bible.

Churches of Quakers: Quakers believe in the authority of Christian Scripture, some of them put greater emphasis to the authority of immediate guidance of the Holy Spirit. Brief introduction to Quakerism – Quakers arises out of a radical interpretation of Christianity that understand Christ according to George Fox, the founder of the movement - he believed that Jesus Christ teaches the people called "Group Friends" about God by himself. The foundational belief of Quaker movements - their faith and practice is that God is knowable by every human being, and that the Spirit of God will lead people into all truth if people are faithful in hearing and obey God's voice in their hearts, that people have the ability to know the truth about God in their hearts as well as be able to discern the will of God for their lives. Quakers believe that not only people of the world were able to know the will of God, but through the grace of God they were empowered to do the will of God.

They believe that Jesus Christ is a living reality in personal experience, not only in the Bible and church tradition. They believe that through an inward experience of the Spirit of Jesus Christ that is available to everyone who Quakerism is not an individualistic, they believe that God speaks to them as a group when they gather together with the intention to receive God's will together. They believe that they were all Groups of Friends fully faithful to God. Quakers believe that all life has the potential to be sacramental, embodied and experienced in every area of life.

Friends – Quakers focus on God's presence and God's activities in every moment of their lives. Quaker's doctrine is social testimonies, religious testimony, Peace Testimony that means putting down earthly weapons and relying only on the power of God's love, and trusting in God's justice. Testimony of Simplicity – God should be centered and be the orderer of their lives. Testimony of Equality – This emphasizes the fundamental brotherhood, and sisterhood of all people. Quaker's practice and their form of worship are based on their faith and openness to the Holy Spirit; Silent Worship and Programmed worship, worship in silence by sitting together for one hour, or two hours or more based on expectant silence waiting on the Spirit of God to work in their hearts and praying that God gives the message.

Quakers are Christians, centered in liberal friends that are in general agreement with Universalists as their role of belief and practice. Fundamentalist's friends can be found in the Evangelical Branch, or in the Orthodox brand. Branches are: conservative, evangelical, holiness, Liberal and Orthodox. Faith expressed a doctrine, through witness – inward and outward expression of faith. Their faith expressed as doctrine in that they believe God is the Creator and sustainer of the universe, God's revelation in Jesus Christ, God's word manifest in Christ, virgin birth, sinless true God and perfect man, Christ is the Word and the Light, the Redeemer. God's revelation by the Spirit – source of God's truth, God's Spirit teaches through the Scripture. God's revelation in the Scripture – in the Old Testament and in the New Testament given is by inspiration of God. Human redemption – God created male and female in his own image, Baptism with the Holy Spirit. Inward promise of the Holy Spirit. An experience where believer's are immersed in Jesus Christ's power, purity and wisdom. The Quakers or the religious Society of Friends called Quaker Baptist Church's doctrine says that the Church is people who through repentance of faith gave their life to Jesus Christ, and were born into His Kingdom with the Holy Spirit into one body.

It was established when the people within the Church of England saw corruption and false doctrine rise in that body in the year 1650. Some Quakers, congregants and members support and affirm Gay marriage, but some members reject Gay marriage – Quakers practice spiritual discernment.

<u>Churches of Shakers:</u> The Shakers were formally the united society of believers in Christ's second appearing, Christian's that combined elements of Quakerism and Charismatic worship practices. Their belief is that all congregants are allowed to prophesy and all prophecies are inspired. Shakers broke off from the Quakers in 1747 in England. Their name formally was shaking Quakers; they were influenced by French Charismatics who fled to England in order to avoid persecution. Founders of Shakers were James and Jane Wardley, former Quakers who claimed that they received a divine command from God to start one true Church. While in England the Shakers were imprisoned for violence, disturbing the peace when services of other churches were going on. They also persecuted them for their beliefs. Eight members of Shakers migrated to the U.S. in 1774 in order to escape persecution. Shakers basic belief in celibacy, means they taught that sexual intercourse is the root of sin, to include the Christian common confession of sin, separation from the world, rejection of the ordained clergy, and practice of Spirit led worship.

Shakers preached repentance of sin, gender equality according to their doctrine. They believe that God is both male and female. The leader of the Shakers, Ann Lee, claimed that she received revelation from God that sex was evil, as a result of abstinence was necessary in order to prepare people for Heaven; where there is no marriage; Jesus Christ is the leader of the first Christian Church. The Holy Spirit is Jesus Christ, Second coming of Christ. Mother Ann Lee believed that she was the female manifestation of God; salvation is based on obedience. Shakers believe in circumcision, Mosaic Law, the way of the Cross and God's new Kingdom. Worship service included prophesying and speaking in tongues. They live in a community and remove themselves from worldly influences, men and women lived segregated and come together in the day to worship and work. Shakers are known for their inventions and woodworking, other than their religion. Shakers' designs were part of a great architectural movement known as Craftsman or Arts and Crafts which emphasized strong, high quality workmanship, natural materials made furnishings are functional unostentatious. Shakers inventions includes circular saw, the clothe pin, modern broom and many items people are using today.

The Shakers are a legalistic cult developed by a deceived, emotionally wounded woman. The doctrine of Shakers are wrong because the Spirit of the Lord that says be fruitful and multiply and fill the Earth will not tell them not to have sex for the co-habitation, people should avoid the theological beliefs of the Shakers. And most importantly, the Holy Spirit will not influence any one to prophesy against the Scripture. God gave Abraham and Sarah grace to conceive Isaac, the child of promise in their old age.

Therefore, we have all different denominations with different beliefs and doctrines from early Christianity until today. The Lutheran denomination was named after Martin Luther and it was based on his teachings. The Methodist denomination got their name because of their founder, John Wesley, who was famous because of his teaching methods of spiritual growth. Presbyterians are named after their church leader Presbyterians. Baptists got their name through their emphasis of baptism.

All have different doctrines and different forms of Baptism, the Lord's Supper, free will and sovereignty of God's doctrine in the matter of salvation. These different denominations are the cause of disagreements over the misinterpretation of Scripture. Disagreement of the Word of God, teaching of Christ, which is taken personally and which becomes as a respect to the point of contention. Denominational churches cause people's personal agendas, self-interest, which also cause self-destruction in the body of Christ. Many churches have a Man-Made denominational creeds over what was written in the Scripture.

Grace D. Balogun

"Everyone who believes that Jesus is the Christ is born of God, and everyone who loves the father loves his child as well. This is how we know that we love the children of God by loving God and carrying out his commands" (1st John 5: 1-2). Genuine faith in the Lord will express itself in gratitude to and love for the Father and for Jesus Christ His son. Faith and love are inseparable, for when we are born of God, the Holy Spirit pours the love of God into our hearts.

Chapter Thirty - Eight

Denominational Churches Observed Holidays & Festivals

January 1st - Feast of St. Basil (Orthodox Christians) - St. Basil died on January 1st, Orthodox Church celebrate this feast of circumcision of Christ on that day. Anglican Church celebrates the Feast of St. Basil on January 2nd, Episcopal Church celebrated it on January 14th, Eastern Orthodox Church, Lutheran Church and Anglican Churches celebrate the Feast of Circumcision of Jesus Christ.

January 1st - Catholic Church Pope celebrates the Feast of Mary motherhood of Jesus Mother of God. Solemnity of Mary - the mother of God.

January 6th - Epiphany (western Christianity) celebrates the revelations of God the Son a - human being in Jesus Christ Western Christians commemorate principally (but not solely) the

Grace D. Balogun

visitation of the biblical Magi to Baby Jesus and Jesus physical manifestation to the Gentiles.

January 6th - Feast of Theophany (Eastern Christianity) on this day, Eastern Christians commemorate the Baptism of Jesus in the Jordan River seen as His manifestation to the world as the Son of God. Greek Orthodox swimmers will hold wooden crosses in the Biospheres Rider's Aden Horn after Mass as part of their celebrations of the epiphany day at the Church of Fenner Orthodox in Patriarch in Istanbul. According to Orthodoxy's faith they uses the old Julian calendar in which Christ was fall 13 days after the Gregorian calendar December 25th.

January 6 - Nativity of Jesus (Armenian orthodox Christianity on this day the Armenian orthodox Christians celebrate the birth of Jesus In connection with Epiphany. Where Priest Orthodox Priests take part in a Christian as procession at the Manger Square outside the Church of Nativity the traditional birthplace of Jesus Christ, in the West Bank City of Bethlehem on January 6th again Orthodox faith uses the Old Julian Calendar. In which Christians falls 13-days after in which Christmas the regular calendar.

January 7th - Christmas Day (Orthodox Christians at a Church in Gaza where Christ was born in Bethlehem.

All Churches Be One

January 19th - Tinkat (Ethiopian Orthodox Christians) Addis Ababa, Ethiopia - Orthodox Patriarch Paolo Abuna Timgat or Epiphany celebration on Tir according to the Ethiopian Calendar which is 12 days after Orthodox Christmas. It is the greatest of the Christian Festivals and celebrates the Baptism of Jesus Christ by John the Baptist in the River Jordan.

January 25th - Conversion of St. Paul (Christian) - The conversion of St. Paul the Apostle, as stated in the Christian Bible, the reported event that took place in the life of Paul of Tarsus which let him to cease persecuting the early Christians and also made him to become a follower of Jesus Christ dated Pope always lead the celebration of the conversion of Saint Paul every January 25th solemnity of the conversion at St. Paul Basilica outside the Walls of Rome.

February 2nd - Christians in Mexico City celebrate every February 2nd of the year caring Baby Jesus Picture as a day that Mary and Joseph took baby Jesus to the Temple in Jerusalem as 40-days after His birth.

February 11th - feast Day of Our Lady of Lourdes (Catholic) marks the day in 1858 when St. Bernadette had her first vision of the blessed Virgin Mary.

Grace D. Balogun

March 3rd - Christian Orthodox dance and celebrate the beginning of Lent.

March 5th - Ash Wednesday (Catholic) worshipers receive ashes during Ash Wednesday to mark the beginning of Catholic Lent pulling the sign with ashes on their foreheads as a sign of repentance which occurs 40-days excluding Sundays, before Easter.

March 16th - Purim (Judaism) Israelites celebrates Purim with their children with special customs and parade in the City of Hebron West Bank - Purim - commemorates the salvation of the Jews from the Ancient Persians according to the Book of Esther.

March 14th - St. Patrick Day (Catholic, Lutheran, Orthodox, St. Patrick's Day is a religious holiday celebrated internationally on March 17 which commemorate Saint Patrick (AD 387-461) the most celebrated Saint in Ireland, observed by Lutheran, Catholic, Anglican, Eastern Orthodox Churches of island.

March 25th - Annunciation (Christian) Catholic Mark the day that Angel Gabriel announce the birth of Jesus to the blessed Virgin Mary. That she will conceive the Son of God.

April - 13th - Palm Sunday (Christians) Christians pilgrims carry palm branches during Palm Sunday procession from Mount Olives into Jerusalem, Old city marking the triumphant of Jesus to Jerusalem cheering crowd greeted Him and shout Hosanna waiving palm leaves the week before crucifixion.

April 15-23 - Passover (Jewish) Jewish men will wrapped themselves with prayer shawls attend the annual cohanim prayer, or priests' blessing for the Pesach (Passover) holiday at the Western Wall in Jerusalem's old City. Jews makes the pilgrimage to Jerusalem during Passover Pesech with commemorate the Israelites exodus from Egypt some 3,500 years ago.

April 17 - India celebrates the Holy Thursday (Catholic) service at St. Anthony's Church Hyderabad. To commemorates the example of Jesus washing the feet of His apostles at the Lord's Supper before His crucifixion.

April 18th - Good Friday (Christians) French bishop - carry the wooden cross to the Mountmarte Basilica during Good Friday to commemorate the death of Christ.

April 19th - Holy Saturday (Catholic Christians) a day before Easter Last day of the Holy week to commemorate the day Christ body laid in the tomb at St. Peter's Basilica at the Vatican.

Grace D. Balogun

April 20th -- East (Western and Orthodox Churches in Pakistan and around the world pray during an Eastern Mass at Church in Lahore - Pakistan - celebration of Holy Week, crucifixion and the resurrection of Jesus Christ.

May 29th - Ascension of Christ (Catholic Christians) Ascension Day marks, the last earthly appearance of Christ after His resurrection. Celebrated 40 - days after Easter.

June 4-5 Shavuot (Jewish) are the African Hebrew Israelites who moved to Israel in 1969 from US, they maintain their culture and were given permanent resident but the Jewish did not recognize them even though they have full knowledge of Torah - vibrant culture means they maintain special diet President in 2003

June 8th - Pentecost (Christians) The Seventh Day Commemorate the descent of the Holy Spirit upon the disciples and the birth of Christian Church on Earth.

June 15th - Trinity Sunday (Christians) marks the first Sunday after Pentecost, Christians meditate on the nature of "God as Three in One" - Father, Son, and Holy Spirit.

June 29th - St. Peter and St. Paul's day (Christians observed the Martyrdom of both Peter and Paul Catholic, Anglican, Eastern Orthodox and Lutheran Churches it is one of the oldest saints day.

July 22nd - Feast of Mary Magdalene (Christians Catholic) Catholic, Lutheran, Eastern Orthodox consider the first person that see Jesus after the resurrection a Saint (Wrong only Jesus Christ is to be worship)

August 5h - Tisha Bav. (Jewish) observation of the destruction of the Temple BC 287 and AD-70 by Roman - Book of Lamentation for the observation - Jerusalem Old City, Jews around the world.

August 6th - Russian Orthodox celebrate the Transfiguration of Jesus Christ in the New Testament on the Mount of Olives. Believers carried the cross walk pass basket of apple salvation.

August 15th - Catholic - Catechism the Assumption feast celebrate virgin Mary's ascent into Heaven St. Nicholas du chardommnet fundamentalist Church 17 Paris(Christ is the only one hat ascend to heaven)

August 15th - Greek Orthodox Priest carried icon of Virgin Mary along the Narrow Street of Jerusalem Old City processions Mark it as (God bearer)

September 8th - Orthodox Christians Mark the birth of Virgin Mary - Catholic, Anglican birth of Mary (Mary is not sinless -

Only Christ Jesus is only that came to earth sinless and lived on Earth sinless.)

September 25-26 - Rosh Hashanah (Jewish) ultra -Orthodox Jews offer prayers in Ukrainian City and around the world to pay homage to their spiritual leader and celebrate the start of New Year at his grave (Rabbi Nachman - 24,000 followers)

November 30th - Advent Sunday (Christians) Marks the start of the advent season, period of waiting of the coming of Christ in England. Started with darkness and lighting of 1,300 candles bright light.

December 8th - Feast of immaculate conception (Catholic) - Catholic the day Roman Catholic remember Mary's conception as being without sin, therefore she is immaculate - Only Christ lives on the Earth sinless, because he was conceived of the Holy Spirit, while Mary had an earthly father and mother.

December 17th - Hanukkah (Jewish) Hanukkah known as the festival of lights, is an eight day Jewish holiday marking the rededication of the Holy Temple in Jerusalem. The national menorah is lit for the first night on Hanukkah on the National Mall, Washington DC on 12/20/2010.

Dec 24th - Christmas Eve (Christian) the night that is before Christmas day when churches all over the world hold services in anticipation of Christmas Day.

December 25th - Christmas Day (Christians) Marks the start of the 12-day Christmas season when Christians celebrate the birth and coming of Christ into the world. Christians and all people gather into the manger Square the central Plaza next to the Church of the Nativity to celebrate the Christmas in West Bank City of Bethlehem, the over the site where Christians believe Mary gave birth to Jesus in a stable, and laid Him in an animals' feeding bough, or manger.

Grace D. Balogun

"This is the one who came by water and blood, Jesus Christ. He did not come by water only, but by water and blood. And it is the Spirit who testifies, because the Spirit is the truth. For there are three that testify the Spirit, the Water and the Blood. And the three are in agreement, We accept man's testimony, but God's testimony is greater because it is the testimony of God which he has given about his Son" (1st John 5:6-8) Love for other people in this world is the second greatest commandment is genuine Christian love if it is accompanied by love for God the first and greatest commandment. Let us love one another as Christ loves us.

Summary

All the denominational churches in the world must review their doctrine and conserve it together into one form of worship for the glory of God. "There is one body and one Spirit - just as you were called to one hope when you were called - One Lord, One faith, One baptism; One God and Father of all, who is over all and through all and in all" (Ephesians 4: 4-6). This is very essential to all the believing Christians' faith and for their unity in Christ. There is only one Lord Jesus Christ; His redemptive work is perfect and sufficient in the universe, no one before Him and there is no one after Him. He is the only begotten Son of the Father full of grace and truth. There is no other Redeemer; Christ is our redeemer King and he is the mediator of a new covenant, Christ is the one that gives all the believing Christians in the world complete salvation. All believers must draw near to God through faith in Christ alone. Jesus Christ is one Lord means that to profess equal or greater allegiance to any authority either in a secular community or religious community other than God revealed in Jesus Christ and it is His inspired Word which is the same as with drawing oneself from Christ's Lordship and thus from the life that is in Christ alone. There will be no Lordship of Christ or the unity of the Spirit apart from the affirmation that the Lord Jesus is the ultimate authority for the believer and to make sure that Christ's authority is communicated in God's written Word. Apostle Paul teaches that the unity of faith and the unity of the Spirit must be perfected by accepting only the faith and the message of the apostle, prophets, evangelists, Pastors, Ministers, Preachers and teachers grown in grace, and advancing toward spiritual maturity as well as growing up in all the aspects into Christ Jesus and being filled with all the fullness of Christ and God. Believers will be no longer children who accept every wind of teaching, but who instead have knowledge of the truth by which to reject false teachers by holding and speaking the revealed truth of the Holy Bible Scripture in love and in living true righteousness and holiness.

With these in mind, all the denominational churches must have only one doctrine and one form of worship. God the Father, through our Lord Jesus Christ, the only God the Son, who is full of righteousness. Christ is coming back to set up His Kingdom and all eyes shall see Him, all those who believe in Him. Christ is one with the Father; all the believers must be one in Him. Christ is the mediator of a new covenant. Jesus Christ is yesterday, today and forever. He is the Lord of lords, the Kinds of kings, the God of gods, in Him all things consist, everything in Heaven and all the things on the Earth. All the believers are being rooted in the revelation of God's love in Christ which is like a true plant with deep roots in the soul; believers must be established in Christ' love is like a building with strong foundations laid on solid rock. The revelation of the love of Jesus Christ is necessary for a deep, deep sold relationship that issues forth with powerful fruit and life to the glory of God. If all the denominational churches in the world followed the Scriptures and not bears in anything, follow the Scripture correctly, the whole world will be evangelized for Christ in due time in any easy, understandable way. But only when no one diverts and make their own way of worship, or rejects part of the Word of God.

All the denominational churches must go and adopt one doctrine before Christ returns for His Church. They must erase all the Man-Made doctrines and follow step-by-step the teaching and the preaching of their Lord and Savior that was in the Scripture by the apostles and the early Church of Christ. Christ is one, and there is no one other. Christ is the foundation of the Church, the head of the him, who gave their life to Him, who follow His commandment of His teaching and preaching in the Scripture. Not those denominational Churches that took out the Cross, and have something to say to justify why they don't want to see the Cross of Christ anywhere around them. They have never preached the Cross and the work of redemption of God through our Lord Jesus Christ.

Further, many denominational churches forsake the Lord's Supper, claiming that it is only for Christ and His disciples. It does not apply to them today. Many denominational churches did not believe in the speaking in tongues; they believe, there is no Spirit of God speaking in tongues today. The Bible is the Word of God. We were told by the Scripture not to take any word out and not to add any word. All those denominational Churches preach what their congregation wants to hear. Some of them are telling their congregational members to just give God the list of what they want, and God will fill it out. They have thousands of congregations, but they are not making disciples; they are not converting souls into the hands of the Lord. They forget that when God, the Holy Spirit came upon His Church, outpoured in sound and in wind and sign of the flame, they spread His truth a broad, and filled with the Spirit, they proclaimed that Christ is Lord. They forgot that Christ is the one, the Lord who lived on this Earth and died, who also rose from the dead to His eternal throne of God. The Father Almighty's right side, He is the one that filled with the Spirit and the Church is continuing to increase.

The Gospel of god continues from the Old Testament to the New Testament. Jesus Christ our Redeemer King who saves us from our past, present, and future sins on the Cross; on the Cross our salvation is completed. All the false prophets and all the false teachers must stop their games and stop running after money, and only run after the ways that that can bring souls into Him. All the denominational churches must keep the Word of Christ in the unity of faith and in the bound of peace. Jesus Christ's priestly prayers on the night He was about to be crucified were that all the "churches must be one, that all of them may be one. "Father, just as you are in me and I am in you May they also be in us so that the world may believer that you have sent me"(John 17:21). Our Lord and Savior Jesus Christ pray that there will be unity in the churches which is primarily spiritual unity based on living in Christ's knowing and experiencing the love of the Father and the fellowship of Christ, separation from the world; obedience, sanctification in truth; receiving and believing the Word of God and a full desire to bring salvation to the sinner and the lost. Our Lord prays for the unity between the believing Christians with the salvation of sinners. The unity, which Jesus Christ prayed was not for external church denominational union, but the unity, which was based on the one in carrying out the service of the Gospel, exhibiting the character of God and Christ. This is what the people of the world will see and they will believe that God the Father sent Him. The nonbelievers and people of all other religions will see and said: definitely Christ is in those believers or they will say these are the true believers just as they see God the Father in Jesus Christ, and glorified the Father, they will see believing Christians in Christ and they will glorify our Lord Jesus Christ. Therefore, it is His will that no stone be left unturned, for the conviction and conversion of the people in the world. Believers must do their best wherever they are to do their utmost to further the work of salvation of souls. The good fruit of the churches all over the Earth is oneness; which will be an evidence of the truth of Christianity and the sure means of bringing many nonbelievers to embrace the gospel of God. It will also recommend, or open Christianity to the world. The embodiment of Christian believers in one community, in one society will greatly promote Christianity. When people of this world see how good and loving all Christians are they will like to join them. Let us try to make sure that all churches are one, in love, in purity, in teaching of the Gospel, in preaching of the Gospel, in character, in our behavior to others, so that we bring glory to God in the name of Jesus Christ. We will be able to evangelize the entire people of this universe to Christ in the bond of love and peace of God that transcends all understanding and the gospel of God will be preached and will reach the unreachable in their own language. The Lord Jesus Christ will open the gates of Heaven and pour His blessings on all the churches that are one in Him, in Spirit and in Truth. Let all the Churches Be one in Jesus Christ's Holy Name

"I write these things to you who believe in the name of the Son of God so that you may know that you have eternal life. This is the confidence we have in approaching God. That if we ask anything according to his will, he hears us. And if we know that he hears us whatever we ask we know that we have what we asked of him" (1st John 5:13-15). Apostle John declares his purpose in writing this letter; it is to provide God's people with a Spirit inspired authoritative assurance of faith and salvation.

Grace D. Balogun

Prayer for the Churches

God the Father Almighty, You are the maker of Heaven and the Earth, the sea and everything that dwells in it. Jesus Christ the only begotten Son of the Father full of grace and truth, the Holy Spirit ever one God. Lord Jesus Christ you are the foundation, the cornerstone, the Head of the Church. You are the immortal, the invisible and the only wise God. You are the way the truth and the Life; in You all life consists. You said: "Let All churches be one" and you said that: "Blessed are they that have seen," but whose their faith in you is very constant. Lord Jesus Christ you told Apostle Peter that: "You will build your Church and all the gates of hell will not prevail against it. I call unto you; with my spirit, soul and body today and as long as I will live on this Earth to help us with your divine love, mercy, and especially with the authority of your Word, bring great changes to all your denominational churches on this Earth beginning from the largest denominational churches to the smallest, or house churches, cave churches, mountain churches, as well as churches that are under the Earth. Bring them together in one before Your Second

All Churches Be One

Coming, our Lord and Savior, make all the denominational churches to have one doctrine and one form of worship. Pray for your churches on Earth, the prayer that can never be uttered. Jesus Christ you are the same yesterday, today and forever; you are the one and only the foundation of the Church, the only one Church of Jesus Christ the Son of God. You gave Your life to the Church, our Lord. You are the Husband of the Church; we are your Bride. You are the Head of the Church and the Corner-Stone, chosen and precious, binding the churches in one on Earth and in Heaven. You said: " God is a Spirit, and those who worship Him must worship Him in Spirit and in truth" (John 4:24). Our Lord Jesus Christ, You explained this truth to the Samaritan woman that the worship of God must come from our state of mind in which we worship God the Father, with all our efforts and show our concerns to be in the right relationship with you, not only in the object of our worship, but very important in the manner of our worship which was instructed the Samaritan woman that all worshipers must worship God in Spirit and in truth as their character and as their duty. Help all the denominational churches on Earth to be able to worship you and the Father and Holy Spirit in Spirit and in Truth.

Let all those who believe in Thee give their lives to You in Spirit and in Truth. Help all the believers to worship the Father in Spirit and in Truth. Send Your Holy Angels, all the heavenly host, and the body of Christ in Heaven to straighten out all the errors in the doctrine of different denominations around the world. Let them know that you are the ever living God, the Head of the

Church; we are part of your body, your flesh and your bones. Correct all the denominational churches let them be one in You and in one doctrine of the gospel of God. Erase all the Man-made Doctrines that is causing confusion among the body of Christ. You are the God of resurrection and eternal life, there no one before you and one after, continue to help us to build your Church on this Earth and do commission through all the believers on this Earth, perform Your great miracles through us, exhibit Your infinite power through us, exercise Your infinite love through us to the people of this world.

Turn all the false teachers, false preachers, false prophets around let them preach the true Gospel boldly and clearly to all their congregations. They are making thousands of congregations, but they are not teaching the true Word of God that will convert the soul. Lord Jesus Christ, turn all your enemies to your friends. Those nations that they don't want Christians to preach the Gospel of God, turn them around let them be lovers of God and His Gospel. Let your holy name be magnified, glorified, adored in the heart and minds of every living soul on the Earth. Turn evil to good, turn violent to peace, turn wickedness to love, turn jealously and envy to love. Let all the people of this world help each other and help each other beginning from their neighborhoods, cities, states and the entire country and between the nations. Lord Jesus Christ let those who do not know You, seek You and find You; let them give their life to You - Spirit, soul and body, in total surrender to Your Lordship where they can be protected and worship You, who only is the Head of the body.

Empower all the denominational churches to preach, teach with the power of the Holy Spirit. Let the gospel of god be preached to all the people in all the nations and make them alive in You, our living Savior. We are waiting for your return. You are our hope of glory; come quickly Lord Jesus Christ. Continuously forgiving the sinners and the lost, people of all other religions, atheists, and same sex marriages, if they come to you with a repentant heart, hear their prayers and forgive them their sins no matter how gruesome it is, wash them as white as snow. Protect all the Christians that are being persecuted for their faith, let the people of the persecuting nations make a good decision to release the persecuting Christians from their prisons; release them as You released apostle Peter from the prison through your angel. Perform Your miracle, release all the persecuted Christians so that they can come out and continue to serve you in Spirit and in truth with singleness of heart. Lord Jesus Christ fulfill the Great Commission through all the believers, purify us with your Word; Your Word is true.

In you Matchless, Great, Mighty and Holy Name, I pray accept my prayers. Amen, amen, amen.

Grace D. Balogun

"That which was from the beginning, which we have heard, which we have seen with our eyes, which we have looked at and our hands have touched this we proclaim concerning the Word of life. The life appeared, we have seen it and testify to it, and we proclaim to you the eternal life, which was with the Father and has appeared to us." (1st John 1: 1-2) Eternal Life in Jesus Christ can only be found only through faith in and fellowship with Jesus Christ the true Son of God.

All Churches Be One

Songs of Praise

Words By Samuel Stone 1866, Music by Samuel S. Wesley 1864.

The Churches' one foundation is Jesus Christ her Lord; she is his new creation; by water and the word; from heave he came and sought her to be his holy bride; with his own blood he bought her, and for her life he died.

Elect from every nations, yet one over all the earth, her charter of salvation; one Lord, one faith, one birth, one holy name she blesses, partakes one holy food; and to one hop she presses with every grace endued.

Though with a scornful wonder we see he sore oppressed, by schisms rent a sunder, by heresies distressed; yet saints their watch are keeping, their cry goes up, "How Long" and soon the night of weeping shall be the morn of song.

Mid toil and tribulations, and tumult of her war, she waits the consummation of peace forever-more, till with the vision glorious her longing eyes are blest and the great Church victorious shall be the Church as rest.

Yet she on earth hath union with God, the three in one, and mystic sweet communion with those whose rest is worn; O happy

Grace D. Balogun

ones and holy; Lord, give us grace that we, like them, the meek and lowly, on high may dwell with thee.

Biblical Indexes

Genesis 1:1-2, 12:4, 28:18, 22, 28: 20, 31:13, 35:2, 17:9-10, 12:8, 13:4, 24:12, 25:21, 18:22-33, 20:7, 2:3

Exodus 6:6-7, 12:14-15, 15:18, 20:8-11, 23:14-17, 30:7-9, 28:6-7, 20:1-2, 20:11

Leviticus 19:2, 1:7, 16:29, 1:8, 27:30-3220:14

Numbers 27:21

Deuteronomy 9:10, 4:32-40, 31:9-13, 33:8, 20:2, 10:8, 31:9, 27:14-15

1st King 8:11, 8:11, 8:57

2nd King 5:1, 10, 14

1st Chronicles 16:36

2nd Chronicles 5:11-14

Job 1:5, 42:6, 42:8-9, 6:8-9

Psalms 2:7, 115:18, 103:1-2, 86:11, 145:18, 99:1-9, 103:2, 78:12, 92:1, 5:3,
66:13-15

Isaiah 54:5-6, 4:4, 53:12, 42:1, 66:2, 57:15, 14:24-27

Ezekiel 36:25-27, 40:48, 14:3-7, 10:18

Matthew 3:11, 7:19, 16:17-19, 3:7-9, 3:13-17, 26:26-29, 6:24, 23:13, 29, 35, 17:20-2122:16-22, 6:5-7, 8:5-7, 10-12, 17:20-21, 24:24-25, 13:22, 11:28-30

Mark 1:8, 11:15-19, 1:40-45, 2:27-28

Luke 22:19-20, 4:16, 24:1, 7:11-15

John 17:20-21a; 17:1-26, 1:33, 14:17, 20:22, 9:11, 19:34. 3:5, 1:32-34, 4:23-24, 6:35, 14:6, 14:12-14, 14:15-19, 20:21-22, 13:4-5, 13: 14-17, 20:29, 17:21, 4:24

Acts 19.32,39,41, 7:38, 1:5, 11:16, 1:15-17, 20:7, 1:7, 15:1-35, 2:38, 3:16

Romans 12:4-5,8:2-5, 12:1-2, 10:9-13, 6:3-5, 8:9-11, 15:4-6, 4:16-25, 14:1-4, 6:1-4, 1:16-17

1st Corinthians 15:45-46, 3:1-4, 12:13, 10:16-17, 11:27-29, 12:1-11 11:17-22, 12:1, 4-11, 14:27-28, 11:23-26

2nd Corinthians 6:16, 11:2,

Galatians 2:20, 3:1-4, 3:3

Ephesians 5:25-27, 1:4-6, 4:12-13, 4:4-6, 4:1-3, 1:21-22, 4:4-6

Colossians 2:11-12,1:18-20

2nd Thessalonians 1:8-9

1st Timothy 5:10

Titus 3:5-7

Hebrews 10:25, 10:9, 13:15-16

James 2:4

1st Peter 1-7, 2:4-10, 2:5, 1:2

1st John 5:6-12, 3:4-5

Jude 17-20

Revelation 21:1-5

BIBLIOGRAPHY

The New International dictionary of Pentecostal and Charismatic Movements. Grand Rapids, Zondervan by Stanley M. Burgess 5/14/2002.

Orthodox Church 455 Questions and Answers a concise and Comprehensive Handbook on the Orthodox Faith Light & Life Publishing Company by Stanley s. Harakas May, 1988.

Handbook of denominations in the United States, 11th Edition by Craig D. Atwood, Nashville Abingdon Publisher 2001.

Baptists around the World: A Comprehensive Hand Book, Nashville Bradman & Holman 1995 by Waldrin, Albert.

Year Book of American and Canadian Churches by Lindner, Eileen w. ed. 2000 Religious Pluralism in the New Millennia 68 ed. Nashville Abingdon.

Dictionary of the Presbyterian & Reformed Tradition in America by hart, D. grand Mark Noll, Downers grove Illinois, Intervarsity Publishing 1999.

Grace D. Balogun

A History of the Work of Redemption by New Haven Yale University Press, 1989.

Man's Natural Blindness in the Things of Religion Volume 2 by Edwards Carlisle, Penn Banner of Truth 1974.

Prophecy and the Church, by Nattley Presbyterian and Redford 1974.

American Indians and Christian Missions Studies in cultural Conflict Chicago: University of Chicago press, 1981.

A History of the Protestant Episcopal Church by Raymond N. Albright MacMillan Publisher 1964.

The History of the Episcopal Church in Frederick, Colonial Anglicanism in North America Detroit Cwayn University Press, 1984.

History of Christianity in the United States and Canada, Grand Rapids, Mich. Eelam, 1992.

Lincoln, c. Eric, and Lawrence Momiya. The Black Church in the African-American Experience. Durham, NC Duke University Press 1990.

Lippy, Charles H, and Peter Williams, eds. Encyclopedia of American Religious: studies of Traditions and Movements 3-volumesNY Scriber 1988.

Dunn, David, History of the Evangelical & Reformed Church Philadelphia: Westminster, 1961.

Ratt, James D. Dutch, Calvinism in Modern America, Grand Rapid, Mich Eerdmans, 1984.

Schaller Lyle E., The seven Day of Week Church, Nashville: Abandon, 1992.

Miller, Donald E. Reinventing American Protestantism: Christianity in the New Millennium. Berkeley University of California Press, 1997.

Feiler, Bruce. Abraham, A Journey to the Heart of three Faiths Se. Frelianlisco Harper Collins, 2002.

Catholic Holy Bible by Bishop Richard Challoner Baronius Press Ltd Edition Dec. 12, 2008.

The Little office of the blessed Virgin Mary 1, 2009 by Roman Catholic Church Author John Newton.

Grace D. Balogun

True Devotion to Mary by Louis De Monfort Roman Catholic Church Baronius Press 1st Ed. 10/1/2008.

Protestant Empire and the making of the British Atlantic World by Pestana, Carla Gardena University of Pennsylvania Press, 2009.

Divine Intimacy by Fr. Gabriel of St. Mary Magdalen Baronius Press 10/1/2008The Protestant Reformation by Hans Q. Hiller brand – perennial; revised ed. 8/4/2009.

Redeeming the enlightenment Christianity and the Liberal Virtues by Bruce Ward 2/15/2010 B. Eerdmans Publishing Company.

Dictionary of the Old Testament Wisdom, Poetry & Writing by Tremper Longman IVP Academic 6/6/2008.

Dictionary of the Later New Testament & Its Developments the IVP Bible Dictionary Services by Ralph P. martin IVP Academic Publisher 11/4/97.

The Protestant Reformation Book by Hans Hiller brand – Baker and Taylor 1979.

Reformation Europe 1517-1559 by Geoffrey R. Elton the World Publishing Company 1964.

Reading in the History of the Lutheran Church Missouri Synod by Carl S. Meyer 9/1/86 Publisher – Concord Publishing House 9/1/86.

Confessions: History and Theology of the Book of Concord by Charles p Arand, Robert Kolb, James A. Nestingen – Fortress Press 4/1/2012.

Lutheran Theology (doing theology) by Steven D. Paulson – Bloomsburg T & T Clark 1st Edition 4/14/2011
The Orthodox Church New Edition by Timothy Ware 6/1/93 Penguin Books second Edition.

Orthodox Christianity Volume One the History and Canonical Structure of the Orthodox Church by Metropolitan Hilarion Alfreyer St. Vladimirs Seminary Press 2/4/2011.

The Orthodox Under Standing of Salvation by Christopher Benyamin Mount Tabor Publishing First Edition 12/20/13
Introducing Eastern Orthodox Theology by Andrew Louth IVP /academic 10/11/2013.

History of the Episcopal Church Revised Edition by Robert W. Prichard 8/1/99.

Grace D. Balogun

History of Church in England by J. Moorman 6/1/80 Morehouse Publishing.

A Brief History of the Presbyterian Church by James H. Smylie 10/1/96 Geneva Press.

Presbyterian Polity for Church leaders by Joan S. Gray – Geneva Press 6/25/12.

Methodic Doctrine the Essentials Revised by Ted A. Campbell 10/1/2011 Abingdon Press.

United Methodist Beliefs A brief introduction by William H. Willimon Westminster John Knox Press 4/19/2007.

Anabaptist History & Theology by C. Arnold Snyder October 1995 Pandora Press.

An Introduction to Mennonite History A popular History of the Anabaptists and the Mennonites by Cornelius J. Dyck Herald Press 5/1/93.

Creating a healthier Church: Family Systems Theology, leadership and congregational life by Ronald W. Richard 8/1/96 Fortress Press.

The Group Church: keys to Congregational Vitality by Belote, Thom 5/1/2010 skinner House Books.

A History of the Baptist by Robert G. Torbet 10/1/73.

History of Baptist Volume I by John T. Christian create Space Independent publishing 5/10/2013.

The Church of Christ by Edward C. Wharton 6/1/2010 Gospel Advocate Company Publisher.

The New Evidence That Demands a Verdict fully update to answer the Questions Challenging Christians today by Josh McDowell Thomas Nelson Publisher 11/23/99.

A Brief History of Seven Day Adventist by George R. Knight 12/21/2013 Review & Herald Publishing Association.

Foundations of Seven Day Adventist Message and Mission by P. Gerar Damsteegt 4/1/77 Andrews University Press.

Christian People of the Spirit: A documentary History of Pentecostal Spirituality from the Early Church by Stanley M. Burgess 6/25/2011 NYU Press.

Grace D. Balogun

Global Pentecostalism: the new face of Christian social engagement by Donald E. Miller, Tetsunao Yamamori University of California Press (/3/2007).

Evangelical Catholicism Deep-Reform 21 Century by George Weigel 2/5/2013 Basic Books Press.

The History of the first Evangelical Lutheran Church in Pittsburgh, 1837-1909 by Pa. First English Evangelical Nabu Press 6/15/2010.

The Complete Guide Christian Denominations by Ron Rhodes Harvest House Publishers 2005.

All Churches Be One

Books previously Published by the author:
Grace Dola Balogun
by
Grace Religious Books Publishing & Distributors, Inc. New York

Grace D. Balogun

PRAYER THE SOURCE OF STRENGTH FOR LIFE - English Edition

Prayer the Source of Strength for Life is a powerful book that will energize your spirit to pray more and more until the prayer is part of your life and until the gate of Heaven is opened and your prayer is answered. Your prayer life will change your life.

LA ORACION FUENTE DE FORTALEZA PARA LA VIDA
– Spanish Edition.

Dios no's dio el poder de la oracion, quiere que lo usemos; debemos illamar, comunicarnos con el en todo lo que estemo spasando. El espera saber denosotros.

Spirit Power Volumes I and II

Spirit Power Volumes I and II both discuss the power of the Holy Spirit in the lives of believers.

The Power of the Spirit of God begins from the creation of the world up until today. That power will also continue until Christ returns to reign. Hallelujah

THE CROSS AND THE CRUCIFIXION

Our Lord Jesus Christ died on the Cross to bring forth love and compassion. Sin's impact on human life brings all other evil into our world, from one society to another society, from one culture to another.

But in Christ, we are clothed with His holiness. We have the gift of eternal life. The gate of Heaven is open and we are eligible for our inheritance in Heaven.

Hallelujah! Hosanna in the Highest. Jesus Christ paid it all, unto Him all we owe. The Cross of Christ is the Cross of joy, peace, and righteousness to all who believe in Him.

Grace D. Balogun

THREE SIMPLE SOLUTIONS FOR WORLD PEACE

Three Simple Solutions for World Peace is a book that clears all the confusion that many people of the world have been going through for many years. It is a book that gives light and advice to some of the problems that plague the world, and that offers solutions for these problems. It is a book that is full of knowledge, understanding and solutions that will bring some peace to the world.

Justification by Faith Alone in Christ Alone

Justification by Faith Alone in Christ Alone will clear all the confusion of believers' faith in Jesus Christ. Believers will also rejoice in the long sufferings – they will rejoice in their sufferings, afflictions, persecutions, rejections and all various trials that may press in on them because these long-sufferings will help all the believers to be redeemed in Christ.

CHRISTIAN CELL PHONE SERIES:

Christian Cell Phone Godly Wisdom helps readers understand the role of God's wisdom and the importance of obtaining godly wisdom in one's life to produce prosperous results in all areas of life. These areas are critical and include family, relationships and finances. The acquiring of God's wisdom is to be sought after in life and will impact others as well.

Christian Cell Phone God's Favor is designed to give readers knowledge of God's favor from the Old Testament to the New Testament. With an analysis of the favor that was on Jesus, the Son of God, the reader will find that God's favor can completely change one's life and lead others to Christ as well.

Christian Cell Phone God's Anointing takes a look at the anointing on the life of Jesus that includes present day believers in Christ Jesus. This anointing can be applied to all areas of life and can be seen in miraculous ways. The anointing is what makes our life incredible and supernatural, drawing all those who see, to Christ.

JESUS CHRIST THE JOY OF CHRISTMAS

Jesus Christ the Joy of Christmas gives praise and tribute to the child that was born in Bethlehem. Tracing the prophecies of Old about this King that was born, the author gives an account of the sinless Lamb of God who came to take away the peoples' sin from a biblical perspective, who is the real Joy of Christmas.

Grace D. Balogun

PRAYER FOR THE BULLY VICTIMS AND THE BULLY TOO!

Prayer for the Bully Victims and the Bully Too addresses the issue of the bully from the classroom to the home. By the use of scriptural application, the author takes a look at what can be done to help the bully kid and their victims. The author has written several key prayers that readers can use to help either the bully victim or parents who are dealing with a child that has become a bully.

All Churches Be One

I AM THE RESURRECTION AND THE LIFE

I Am The Resurrection and The Life: Powerful, inspirational and written from a firm biblical perspective, multi-published author Grace Dola Balogun, gives life to others through the power of Jesus Christ who is the Resurrection and the life. This book will open eyes to the amazing and abundant blessings of accepting Jesus Christ as your Lord and Savior, giving keen insight into the Scriptures on the power available to all through the Holy Spirit with an emphasis on aspects of eternal life for the believer.

I AM THE ETERNAL LIFE

I Am The Eternal Life: Encouraging, uplifting and filled with a sound biblical perspective, this book encourages believers and non-believers alike to look to the One that is Jesus Christ, the Son of God, who is the Bread of life and the one who gives eternal life to all who believe in Him. This book gives readers a heavenly perspective on their life, revealing believer's God-given destiny and purpose to all who call on Jesus Christ as their Lord and Savior. The truth of the Gospel and the Good News is eloquently displayed in this delightful and insightful read.

HE WHO BELIEVES IN ME SHALL NEVER DIE

He Who Believes In Me Shall Never is a fascinating teaching, revealing Jesus as the way, the truth and the life - the Everlasting life. All who believe in Him shall never die. Beginning from the Old Testament, the author takes a look at the fall of humanity through the sin of disobedience through Adam and Eve. Comparing this fall to the sin of disobedience today, the author reveals scriptural truths in the lives of Enoch, Elijah and Moses. The author gives insight into the baptism of the Holy Spirit and gives examples of the Spirit's power and the purpose for which the power is given to believers. The author has given key scriptural insights that all who believe in Jesus Christ will have everlasting life in Him that continues to Heaven.

Grace D. Balogun

FORGIVE OUR DEBTS AS WE FORGIVE OUR DEBTORS

Forgive Our Debts As We Forgive Our Debtors speaks of divine forgiveness from the Lord and the Lord's commandment to forgive others, including ourselves. With the Lord's Prayer as a foundation, author Grace D. Balogun, explores from the Old Testament to the New Testament meanings of forgiveness and the consequences of sin. The author gives keen biblical insight into the subject of forgiveness, bringing life-changing healing that is only acquired through the power of forgiveness.

She must be Silent: The Great Commission Bestowed on Both Men and Women is a controversial book that takes a look at the role of women throughout biblical history and gives key scriptural insight into the role of women from the Old Testament to the New Testament. An encouraging, enlightening read, this book is recommended for women and men that want to understand the role of women from a biblical perspective. This book does an excellent job in giving insight into key roles that women play in God's redemptive plan and sheds light on the empowerment of the Holy Spirit that is given to both men and women by God, who is no respecter of persons.

Grace D. Balogun

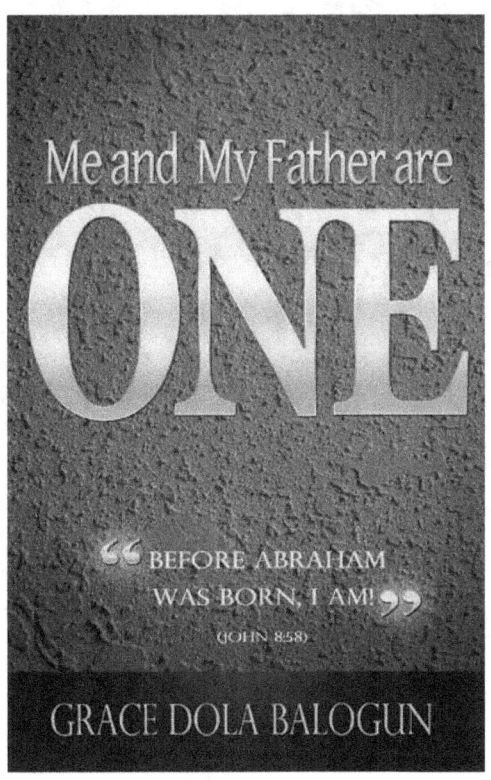

Me and My Father Are One: Before Abraham was Born, I Am (John 8:58) explains that God the Father and Jesus Christ are one from the beginning. In this book, the reader will learn that the plan of redemption is from the Father and is carried out through His Son, Jesus Christ, who is the Word of God. In the beginning, before Abraham, before Adam and Eve, Christ says, "I Am." Written from a biblical perspective, the author displays that Jesus Christ was in the beginning and as Scripture says, "He is before all things, and in him all things hold together "(Colossians 1:17).

The Messenger and the Message of God (Volumes I & 2) systematically offers the message of God spoken through the prophets of Old and Christ's disciples in the gospels, to include the mission of Paul the Apostle. For use as an individual study or within a group setting, these volumes are recommended to gain understanding of certain books of the prophets and the New Testament gospels. *Volume I* is focused on selected prophets of the Old Testament and *Volume II* relates the disciples and their callings in the gospels of the New Testament. God has spoken, is still speaking today and we are to listen to Him, heeding the message.

Grace D. Balogun

Be Holy for I Am Holy - God has created and redeemed all of the Christian believers; we belong to Him, and we have passed through troubles and afflictions. We will not be destroyed, for He is with us. We are precious and honored in His sight; believers are the objects of His great love. God loved us before he put us in the womb and brought us into this world. God will never forsake His people. He would continue His love for they would still be a special people reserved for mercy. The expressions of God's goodwill to His people here speak abundance of comfort to all of the spiritual children of upright Jacob who are praying for Israel. Through God's care and concern for His people, God created the people of Israel especially for Himself. He made them into a people; God incorporated them by His covenant—purchased and redeemed them. It is the same way with those who are redeemed by the blood of His Son, Jesus Christ.

All Churches Be One

Christ's Life in the Life of Christians - This book will help you to understand your position in Jesus Christ as a Christian. Reading this book will also give clear understanding of who Christ is in the life of believing Christians. It will give you more divine ability as well as the power of the indwelling of the Holy Spirit that Christ gave to all who believe and gave their life to Him. Jesus Christ is the one who initiates and the one who establishes the New Covenant and His heavenly ministry is far beyond and far more superior to the ministry of Old Testament priests. The New Covenant is an agreement, promise, the last will and testament and a statement of intention to be bestow divine grace and blessing on all those who believe in God; those who in sincere repentance and through faith accept Jesus Christ as the true Son of God.

Remember the Poor & Needy Among Us will help all the believing Christians to learn how important it is to give to the poor, the needy and the sick. Christians must give part of what God provides for them to increase the work of the Lord on this Earth, to reach the people of the entire world for Jesus Christ in their own language. Christians must set apart for God every day, part of their income, and other natural resources to honor God and to enhance the work of the Kingdom of God on this Earth. They must also give their resources to charity, to the poor, so that the poor may have something to eat and be satisfied. When you make a feast, or doing any celebration, invite the poor and the needy. People who are unable to pay you back because they were unable to work for a living. By feeding them, clothing them, helping them, these types of charity are the true charity.

ABOUT THE AUTHOR

Grace Dola Balogun graduated from Fordham University Graduate School of Religion and Religious Education in the year 2010 with an M.A. in Religion and Religious Education. She has been a prayer mentor and advisor for many Christians of all denominations for many years.

Visit her online at: www.Gracereligiousbookspublishers.com

Grace's Blog: http://author-grace-dola-balogun.blogspot.com/

Facebook - https://www.facebook.com/grace.d.balogun

Twitter - https://twitter.com/prayersource

To order additional copies of this book, please E-mail: info@gracereligiousbookspublishers.com.

This book may also be ordered from 30,000 wholesalers, retailers, and booksellers in the U. S., and in Canada and over100 countries globally.

To contact Grace Dola Balogun for an interview or a speaking engagement, please E-mail:

info@gracereligiousbookspublishers.com

Grace D. Balogun

The Spirit and the bride say,

"Come!" And let the one who hears say, "Come!" Let the one who is thirsty come;

and let the one who wishes take the free

gift of the water of life (Revelation 22:17).

MARANATHA EVEN SO COME LORD JESUS (1ST CORINTHIANS 16:22, REVELATION 22:20)

All Churches Be One

ORDER FORM

TO ORDER YOUR COPY OF ANY BOOK:

NAME:_____

ADDRESS:_____

_____

TELEPHONE:_____

FAX#:_____

MAIL:_____

QUANTITY:_____

MAIL TO:

Grace Religious Books Publishing & Distributors, Inc.
New York
213 Bennett Avenue
New York, NY 10040

Grace D. Balogun

www.ingramcontent.com/pod-product-compliance
Lightning Source LLC
Chambersburg PA
CBHW052013070526
44584CB00016B/1731